SWORDS

Special thanks to Liz Bicknell, James Weinberg, Katie Cunningham,
and the entire Candlewick crew. Thanks also to John Kubasco,
Rosemary Stimola, Terry Tuttle, Jim Leist, and to the friends and
family who helped me along the way.

Beowulf excerpt on page 5 adapted from the translation by Francis B. Gummere
(P. F. Collier & Son, 1910)
Samurai painting on page 52 inspired by an antique woodblock print of
Nitta Yoshisada fighting at the Battle of Fujishima, in *Samurai Commanders*
by Stephen Turnbull (Osprey Publishing, 2005)

First paperback edition 2012

Library of Congress Cataloging-in-Publication Data is available.

Library of Congress Catalog Card Number 2007052333

ISBN 978-0-7636-3148-2 (hardcover)
ISBN 978-0-7636-5098-8 (paperback)

12 13 14 15 16 CCP 10 9 8 7 6 5 4 3 2

Printed in Shenzhen, Guangdong, China

This book was typeset in Historical Fell.
The illustrations were done in digital media.

Candlewick Press
99 Dover Street
Somerville, Massachusetts 02144

visit us at www.candlewick.com

SWORDS

AN ARTIST'S DEVOTION

WRITTEN & ILLUSTRATED BY

Ben Boos

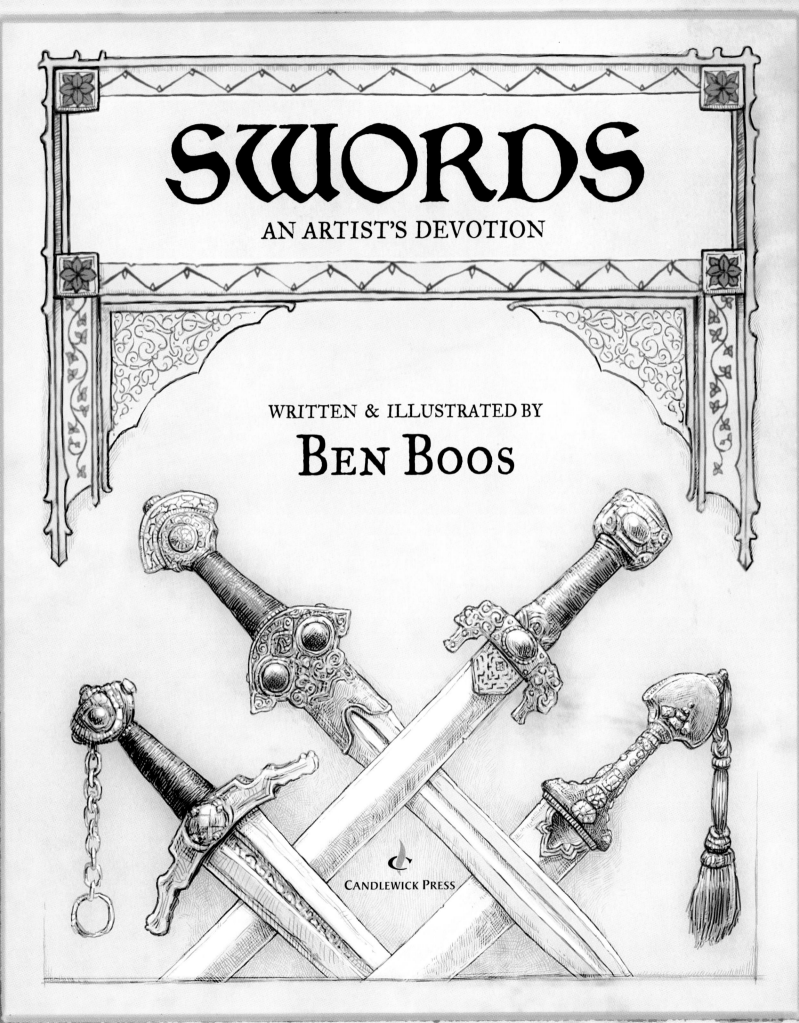

CANDLEWICK PRESS

To my wife and children

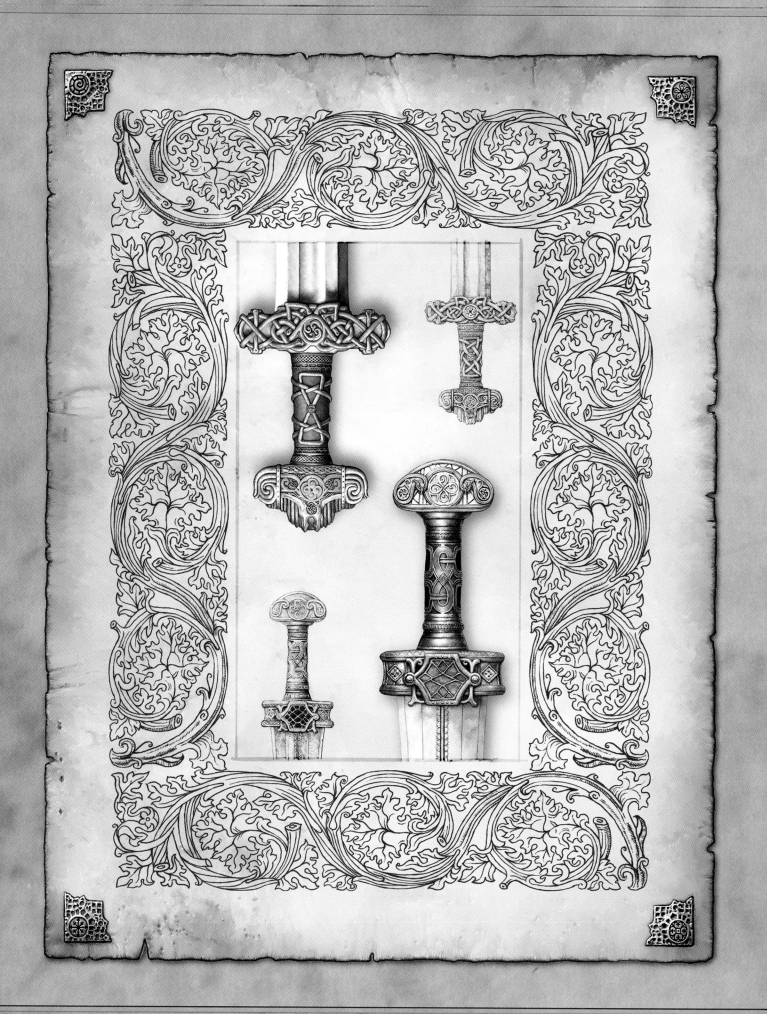

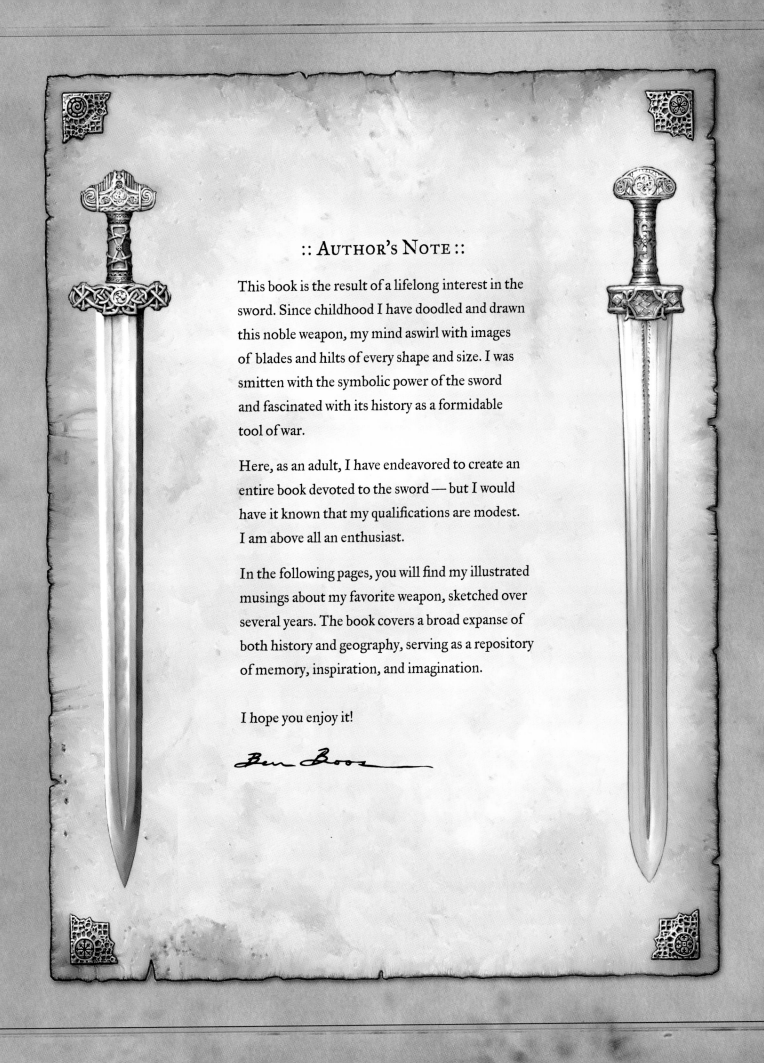

:: AUTHOR'S NOTE ::

This book is the result of a lifelong interest in the sword. Since childhood I have doodled and drawn this noble weapon, my mind aswirl with images of blades and hilts of every shape and size. I was smitten with the symbolic power of the sword and fascinated with its history as a formidable tool of war.

Here, as an adult, I have endeavored to create an entire book devoted to the sword — but I would have it known that my qualifications are modest. I am above all an enthusiast.

In the following pages, you will find my illustrated musings about my favorite weapon, sketched over several years. The book covers a broad expanse of both history and geography, serving as a repository of memory, inspiration, and imagination.

I hope you enjoy it!

Ben Boos

:: Contents ::

1 Warriors 2

2 Raiders 8

3 War Maidens 14

4 Villagers 20

5 Soldiers 26

6 Landsknechts 32

7 Knights 38

8 Kings 44

9 Samurai 50

10 Ninja 56

11 Silla Knights 62

12 Eastern Masters 68

13 War Chiefs 74

14 Sultans 80

CHAPTER —1

WARRIORS

Since the dawn of time, men have taken up the sword in combat. Some among them were so capable that they were considered to be in a class of their own — the mighty warrior class. These men were revered as brave, heroic, and essential to life, for they were the guardians of their people.

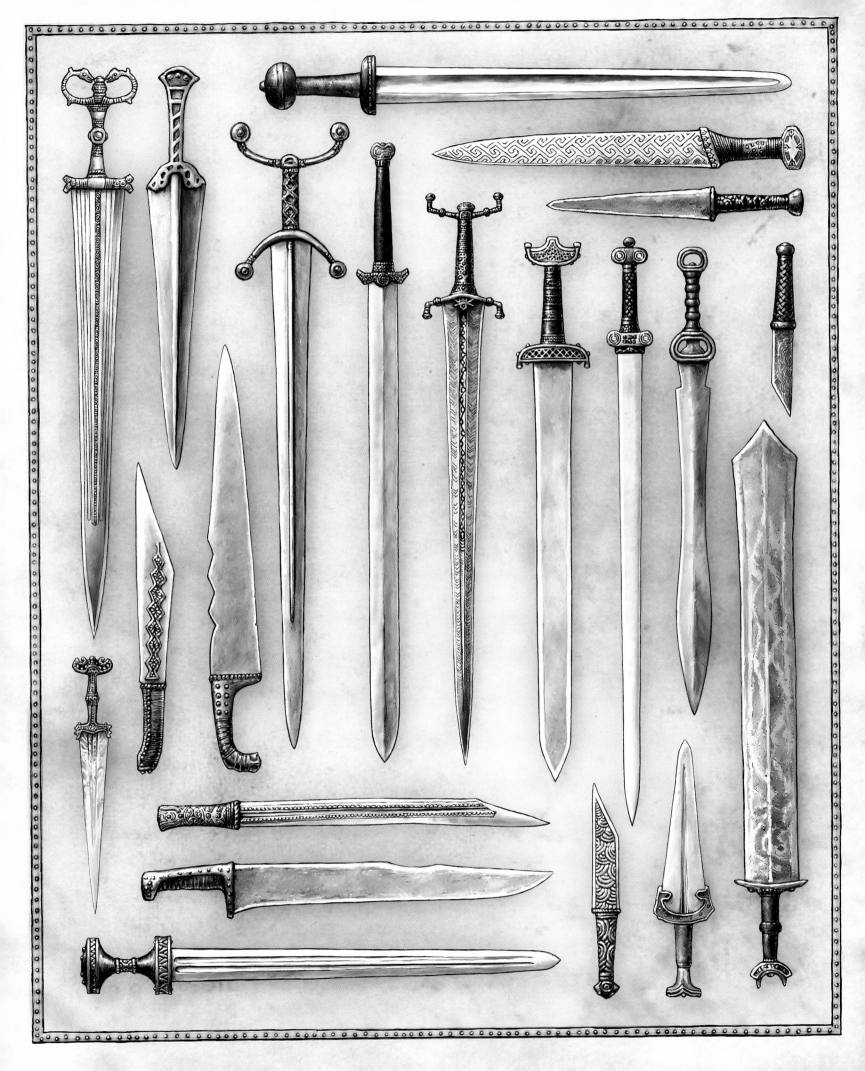

BRONZE AGE SWORDS

To compensate for the weak metals used in the Bronze Age, early swordsmiths devised clever shapes that aided rigidity:

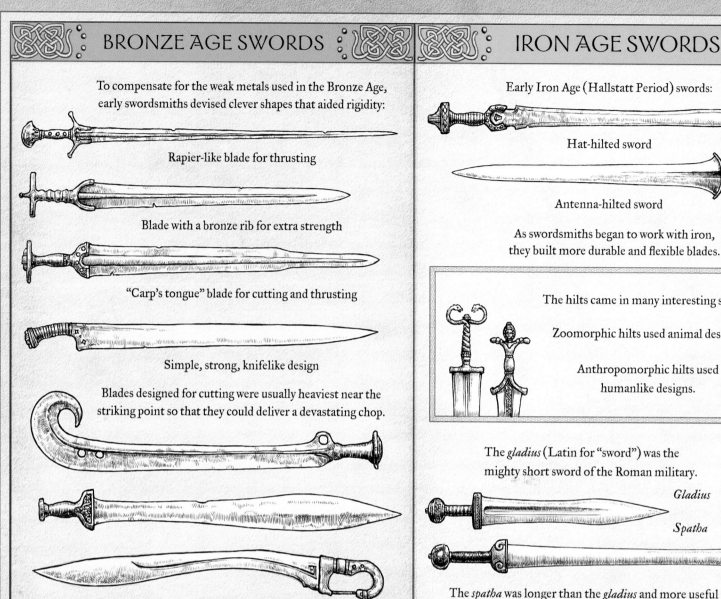

Rapier-like blade for thrusting

Blade with a bronze rib for extra strength

"Carp's tongue" blade for cutting and thrusting

Simple, strong, knifelike design

Blades designed for cutting were usually heaviest near the striking point so that they could deliver a devastating chop.

IRON AGE SWORDS

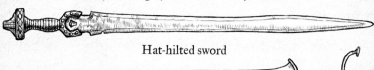

Early Iron Age (Hallstatt Period) swords:

Hat-hilted sword

Antenna-hilted sword

As swordsmiths began to work with iron, they built more durable and flexible blades.

The hilts came in many interesting shapes:

Zoomorphic hilts used animal designs.

Anthropomorphic hilts used humanlike designs.

The *gladius* (Latin for "sword") was the mighty short sword of the Roman military.

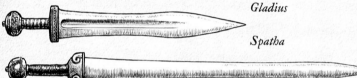

Gladius

Spatha

The *spatha* was longer than the *gladius* and more useful for cavalry.

LA TÈNE–STYLE HILTS

The *La Tène*–style weapons were Celtic swords similar in design to the Roman *spatha*.

MIGRATION-STYLE HILTS

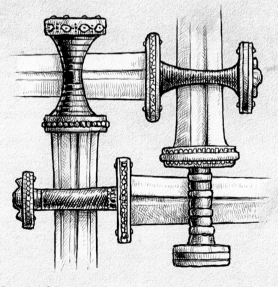

Swords of the migration period (AD 300–700) were transitional designs that prefigured the Viking swords of a later age.

A TALE FROM THE AGE OF HEROES

In the story of Beowulf, we learn of a brave warrior tasked with the slaying of a foul demon. For this dangerous adventure, he traveled into her wicked lair with a fine sword:

It was not the worst of mighty weapons
which Hrothgar offered for his need:
Hrunting they named the hilted sword.
Of old-time heirlooms, it was easily best;
iron was its edge, all etched with poison,
and with battle-blood hardened.
Never had it faltered at fight
in the hero's hand that held it.
Not the first time, this, that it
was destined for a daring task....

With a mighty stroke he swung the sword,
and that seemly blade sang on her head
its war-song wild. But the warrior found
the light-of-battle loath to bite.
Its hard edge failed the noble at his time of need:
The first time, this, for the gleaming blade
that its glory fell....

All was not lost! For in the den of the demon, deep in a cave beneath a lake, Beowulf found a sword from another age — a sword that was a match for the monster:

Amid the battle-gear saw he a blade triumphant,
old-sword of giants, with edge impenetrable,
a warrior's heirloom, a weapon as unmatched
as the monsters who had wrought it.
He seized the sword and so wrathfully smote ...
that the blade pierced her flesh; she sank dead to the floor. *

. . .

* Adapted from the translation by
Francis B. Gummere (1855–1919)

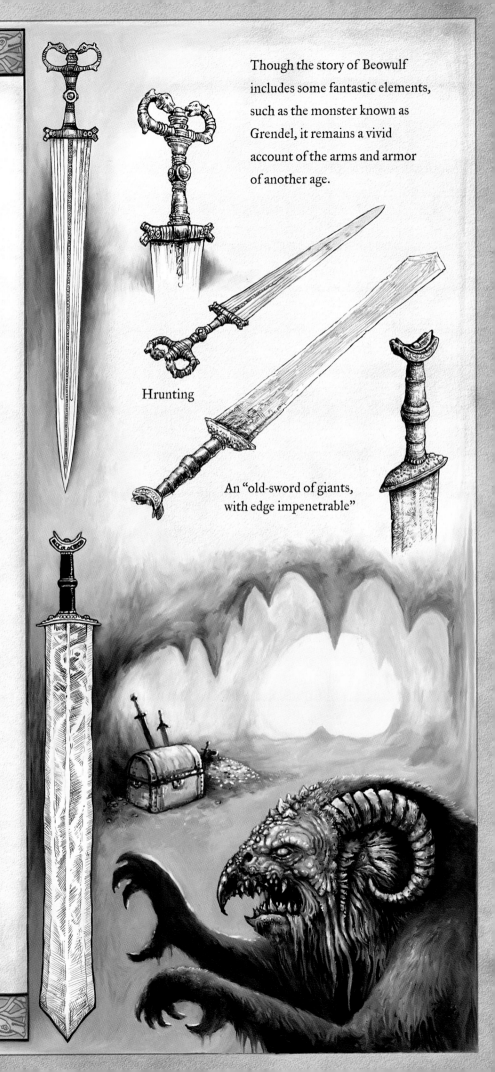

Though the story of Beowulf includes some fantastic elements, such as the monster known as Grendel, it remains a vivid account of the arms and armor of another age.

Hrunting

An "old-sword of giants, with edge impenetrable"

RAIDERS

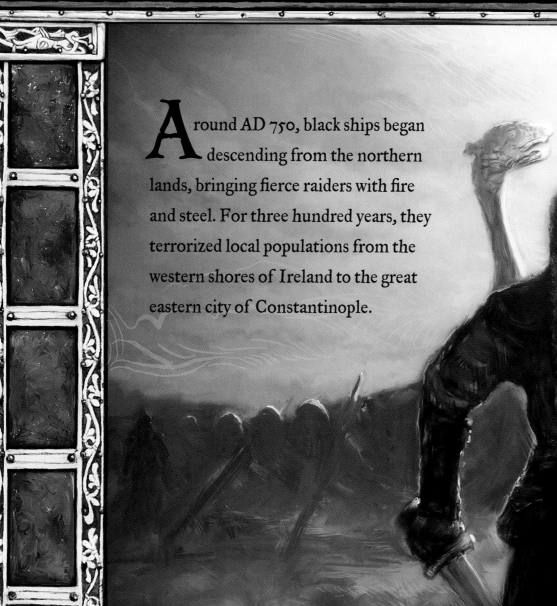

Around AD 750, black ships began descending from the northern lands, bringing fierce raiders with fire and steel. For three hundred years, they terrorized local populations from the western shores of Ireland to the great eastern city of Constantinople.

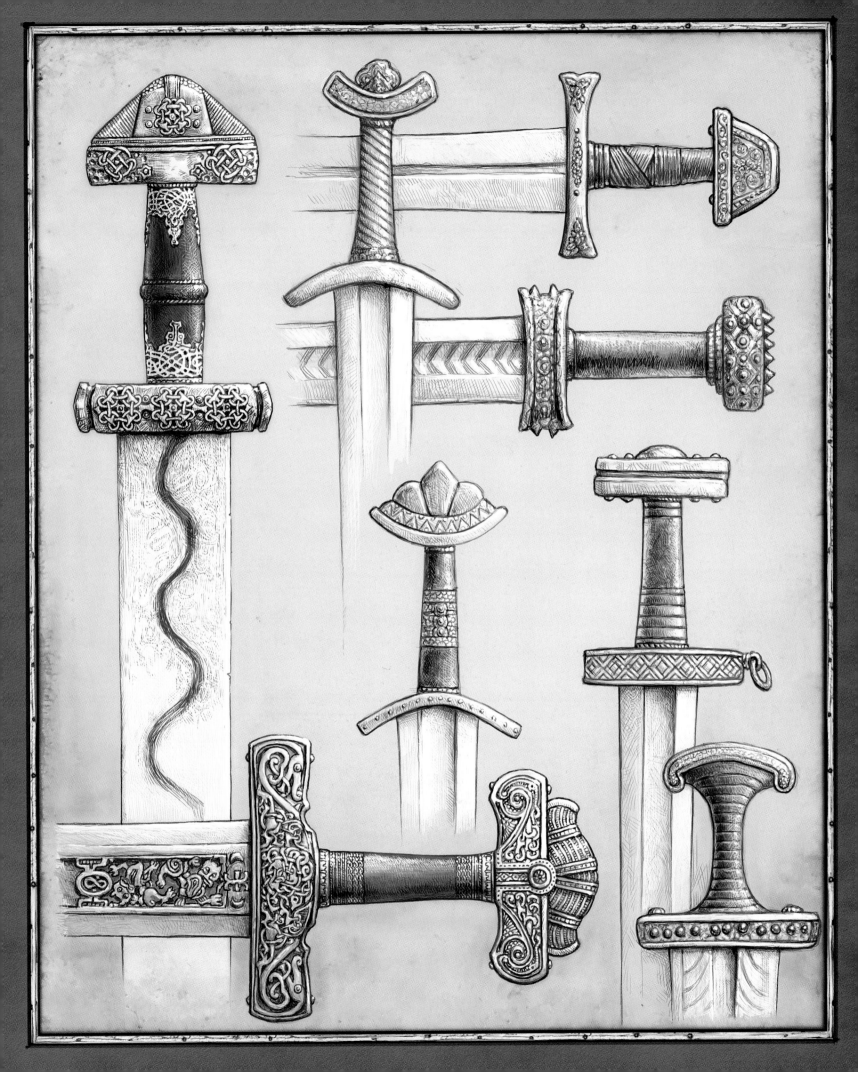

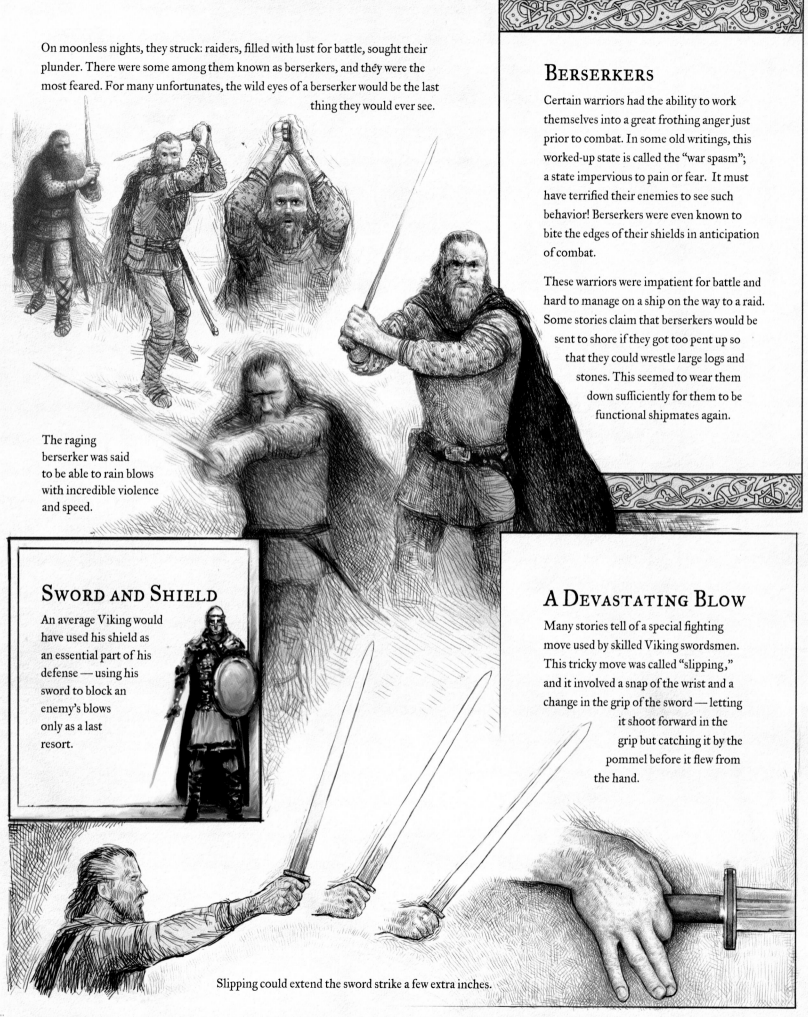

On moonless nights, they struck: raiders, filled with lust for battle, sought their plunder. There were some among them known as berserkers, and they were the most feared. For many unfortunates, the wild eyes of a berserker would be the last thing they would ever see.

The raging berserker was said to be able to rain blows with incredible violence and speed.

BERSERKERS

Certain warriors had the ability to work themselves into a great frothing anger just prior to combat. In some old writings, this worked-up state is called the "war spasm"; a state impervious to pain or fear. It must have terrified their enemies to see such behavior! Berserkers were even known to bite the edges of their shields in anticipation of combat.

These warriors were impatient for battle and hard to manage on a ship on the way to a raid. Some stories claim that berserkers would be sent to shore if they got too pent up so that they could wrestle large logs and stones. This seemed to wear them down sufficiently for them to be functional shipmates again.

SWORD AND SHIELD

An average Viking would have used his shield as an essential part of his defense — using his sword to block an enemy's blows only as a last resort.

A DEVASTATING BLOW

Many stories tell of a special fighting move used by skilled Viking swordsmen. This tricky move was called "slipping," and it involved a snap of the wrist and a change in the grip of the sword — letting it shoot forward in the grip but catching it by the pommel before it flew from the hand.

Slipping could extend the sword strike a few extra inches.

VIKING HILTS

A variety of Viking sword hilts, classified by the wonderful historian Ewart Oakeshott as types 1 through 9

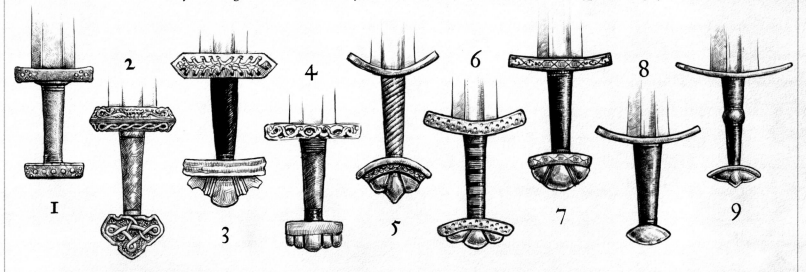

VIKING BLADES Viking smiths created some of the most lethal, no-nonsense fighting tools ever designed.

Single-edged

Double-edged

Short

THE PATTERN WELD

Iron strips of different composition were twisted together and then forged into the core of the blade. By this method, the swordsmith could control the hardness and flexibility of the blade.

THE RING SWORD

Some Viking swords were fitted with a ring on the hilt. The exact purpose of the ring is a mystery.

Perhaps a Viking would bind the sword to its sheath during life at home, to prevent it from being drawn in haste or anger. In certain cases, a sword would be unbound for a duel between rival Vikings.

THE SNAKE IN THE BLADE

The Norse sagas mention a "snake" in the sword that was revealed by blowing on the blade.

Perhaps the moisture of the breath revealed the pattern weld at the core of the blade, which sometimes looked like the markings on a snake's back.

CHAPTER 3

WAR MAIDENS

Throughout the ages, great female fighters have arisen to become champions of their people. Queen Boudicca of Britain was such a warrior: she faced down the overwhelming Roman legions to fight for her people's freedom.

These brave and noble women are written into the sagas and histories, and they prove beyond doubt that the sword in the hand of a war maiden is as fearsome as the sword in the hand of any man.

MAIDENS OF WAR

Around the first century BC, in the distant past of Ireland, legend speaks of a warrior queen known as Maeve of Connacht.

She is an example of a particularly beautiful yet bloodthirsty female warrior of her time.

Vebjorg was a famous shield maiden of Norse legend. Her feats made her the equal of any male champion.

CHAPTER 4

VILLAGERS

The forested heartland of Europe was settled by brave villagers who were able to carve out a rough living from the land. It was a time of grave danger, and these hardy folk used an array of knives to defend themselves from the bandits and beasts of the wood.

This family of knives ranged in size from the small farmer's knife to the giant war knife.

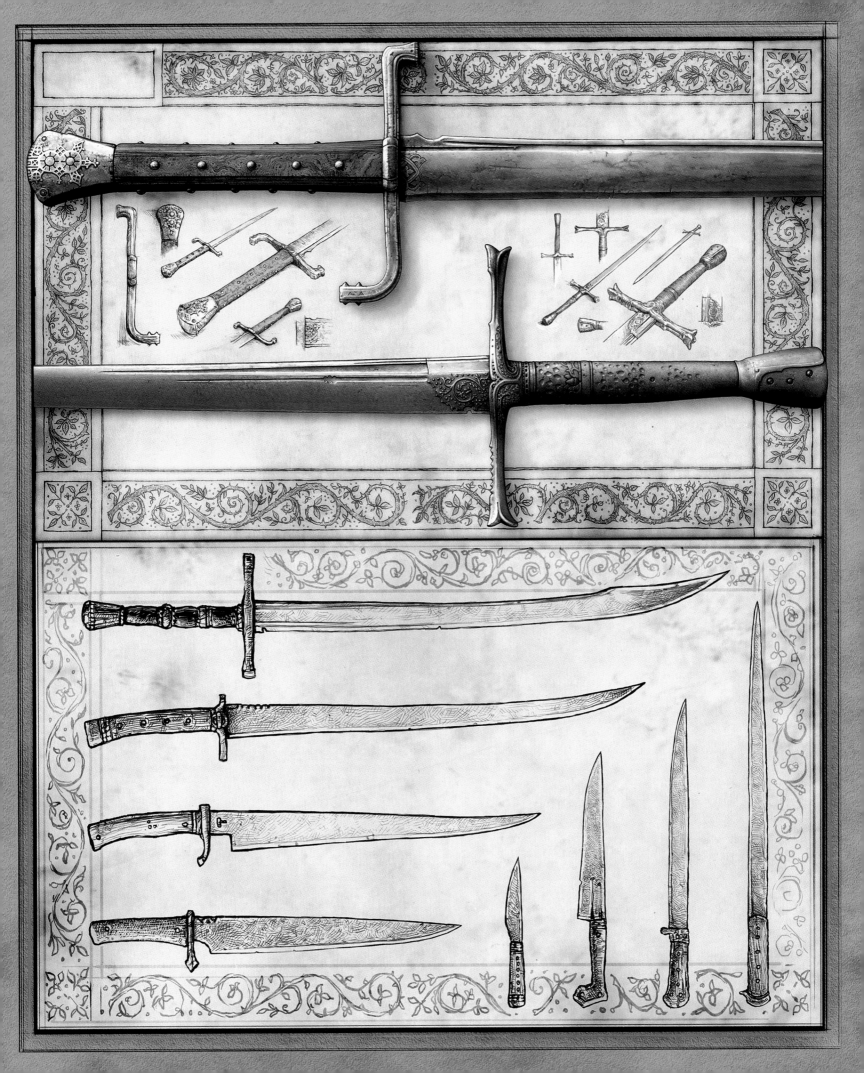

The Farmer's Knife

The farmer's knife was a useful tool for all the tradesmen of a village, whether they were hunters, smiths, woodcutters, or farmers. It was easily made by a local smith, and it served well as a weapon and a tool.

Dangerous Game

Some of the animals hunted in the dense European woods were quite dangerous, including the wild boar, a large feral pig. Especially brave hunters of these tusked beasts favored the sword as a weapon of choice. It surely would have been easier to use a bow or spear, but hunting boars with a sword was considered sporting. It must have taken great skill to fight these beasts at such close range while avoiding being gored by their fearsome tusks. Boars were said to have such bloodlust that, once provoked, they would willingly impale themselves up to the hunter's sword hilt just to get in close enough to deal the hunter a deadly blow.

OFFENSIVE WEAPONRY

There were occasions when villagers would be recruited to fight in a larger war alongside the knights and soldiers of the realm. Short knives were excellent close-quarters weapons, while larger war knives could deliver a devastating chop to all but the toughest armor.

SELF-DEFENSE

The village smiths were also capable of producing larger and more battle-ready weapons, which would have been handy for crossing swords with bandits or invaders.

DEADLY TECHNIQUE

Medieval texts, such as the *Codex Wallerstein*, document some elaborate and graceful fighting moves designed for even the largest war knives.

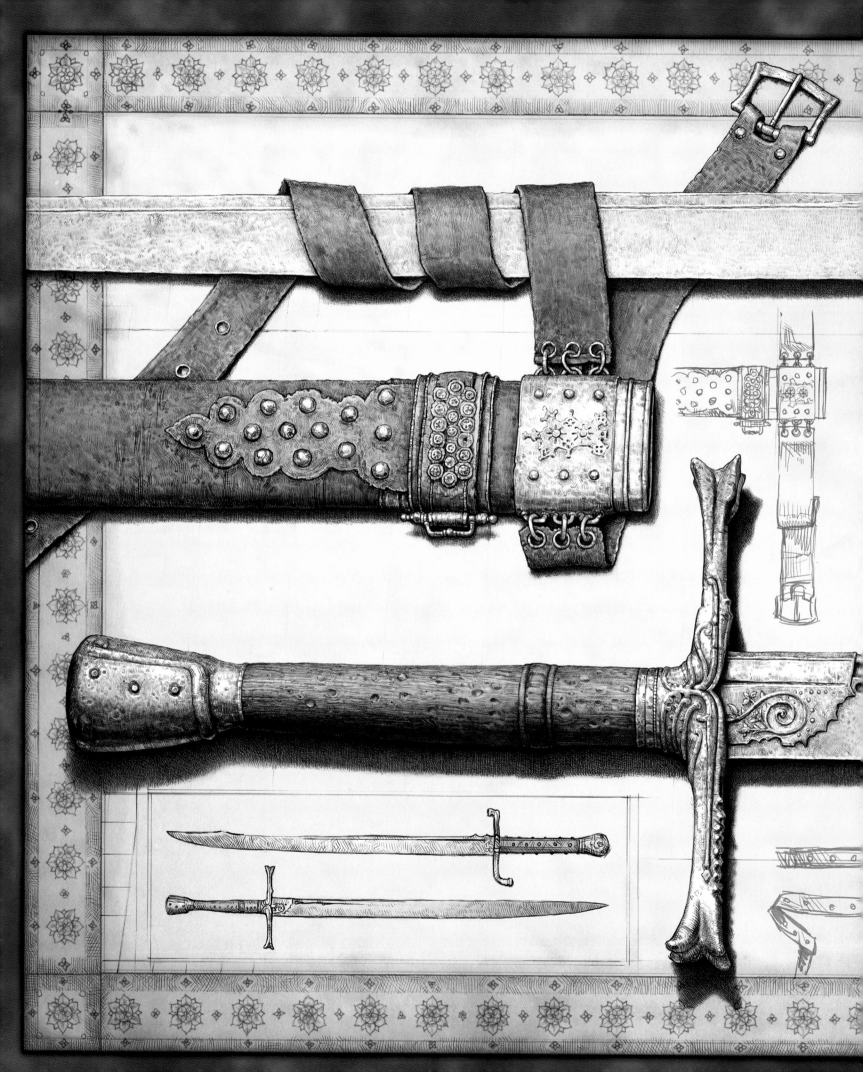

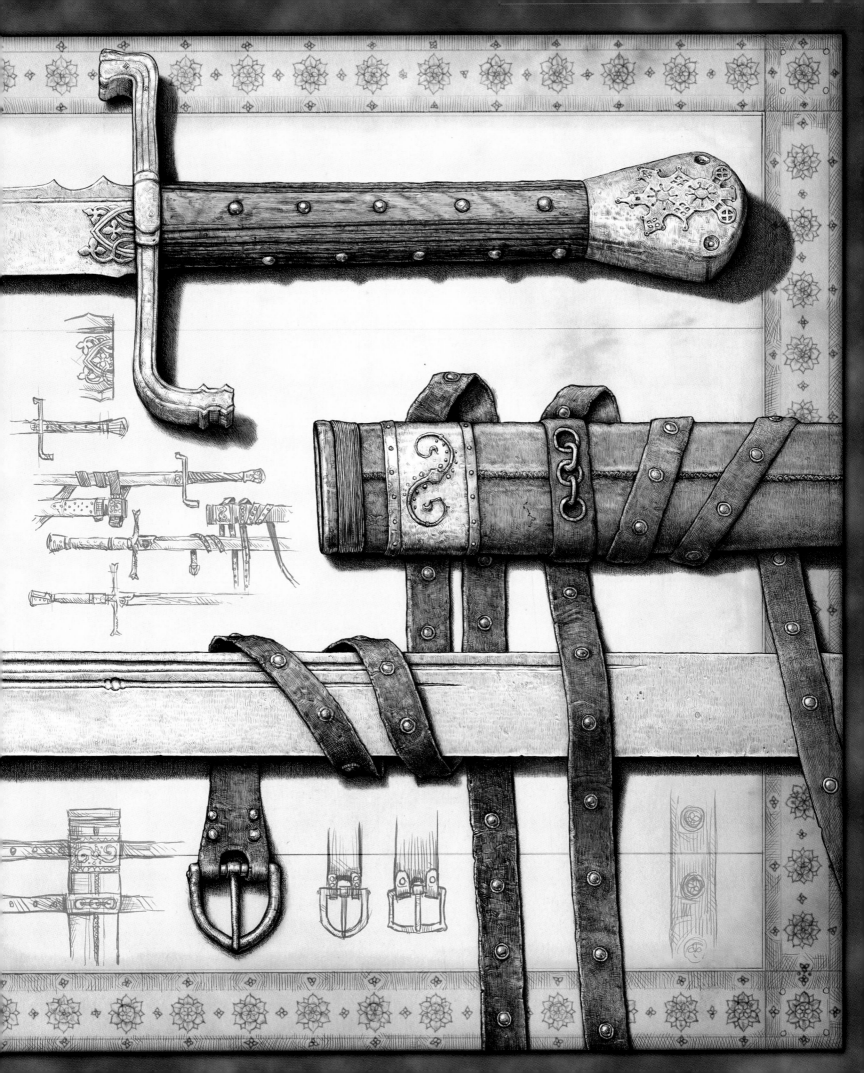

SOLDIERS

Soldiers were the backbone of the medieval army, fighting as infantry alongside cavalry and siege machinery. In large, disciplined groups, soldiers became formidable tactical weapons — especially when trained to fight with swords.

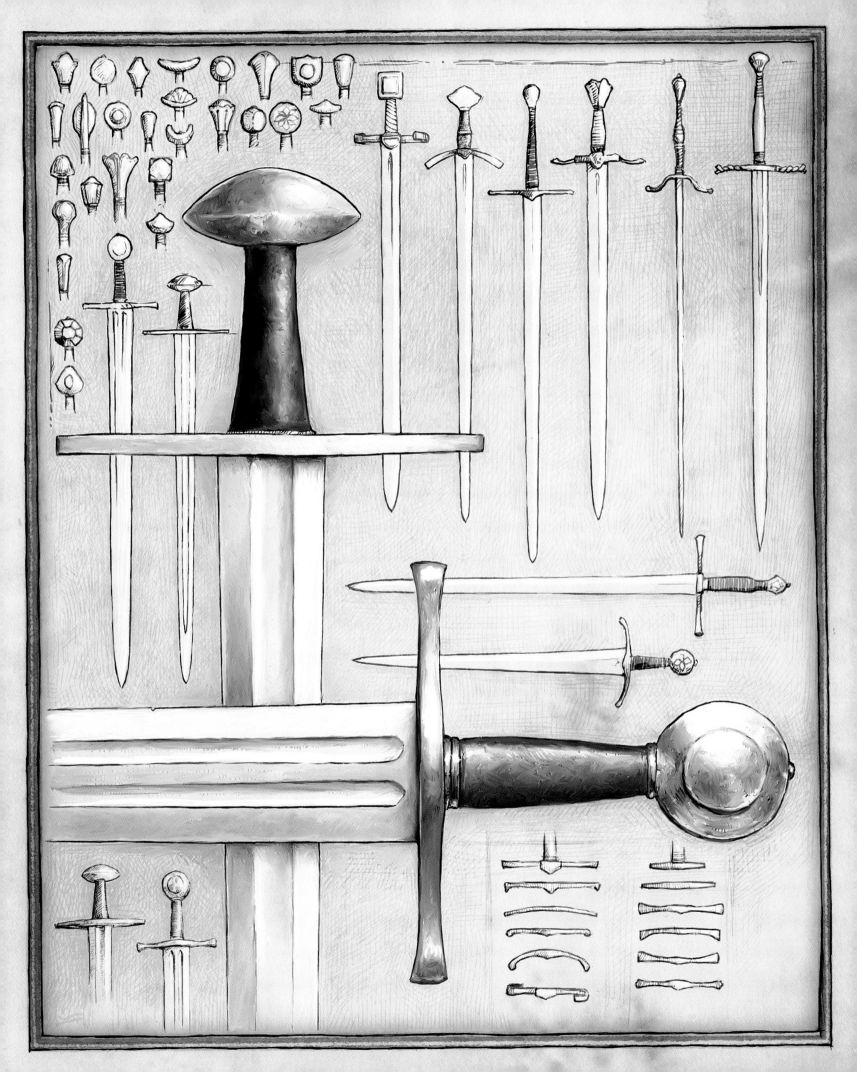

- An ideal sword is light and flexible.

- It should bend, then return to true.

- A light blade allowed a well-trained soldier to strike quickly from a number of positions while maintaining full control over the weapon.

- At almost any point in use, a light blade could be brought about for a defensive block. A block could also turn into a strike.

- A wide cruciform (cross-shaped) *guard* prevented the hand from getting crushed against an enemy's shield, and the *pommel*, a knob at the top of the sword's handle, provided a counterweight so that the user could balance the sword and wield it comfortably.

The historian Oakeshott classified swords into groups depending on the features of the blade.

The swords depicted at right are based on Oakeshott's research of various blade types.

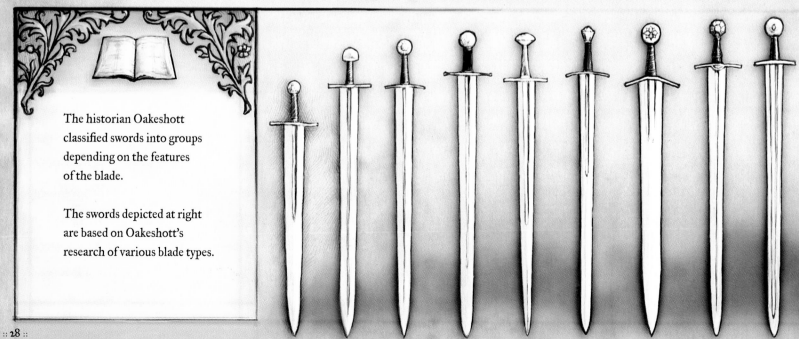

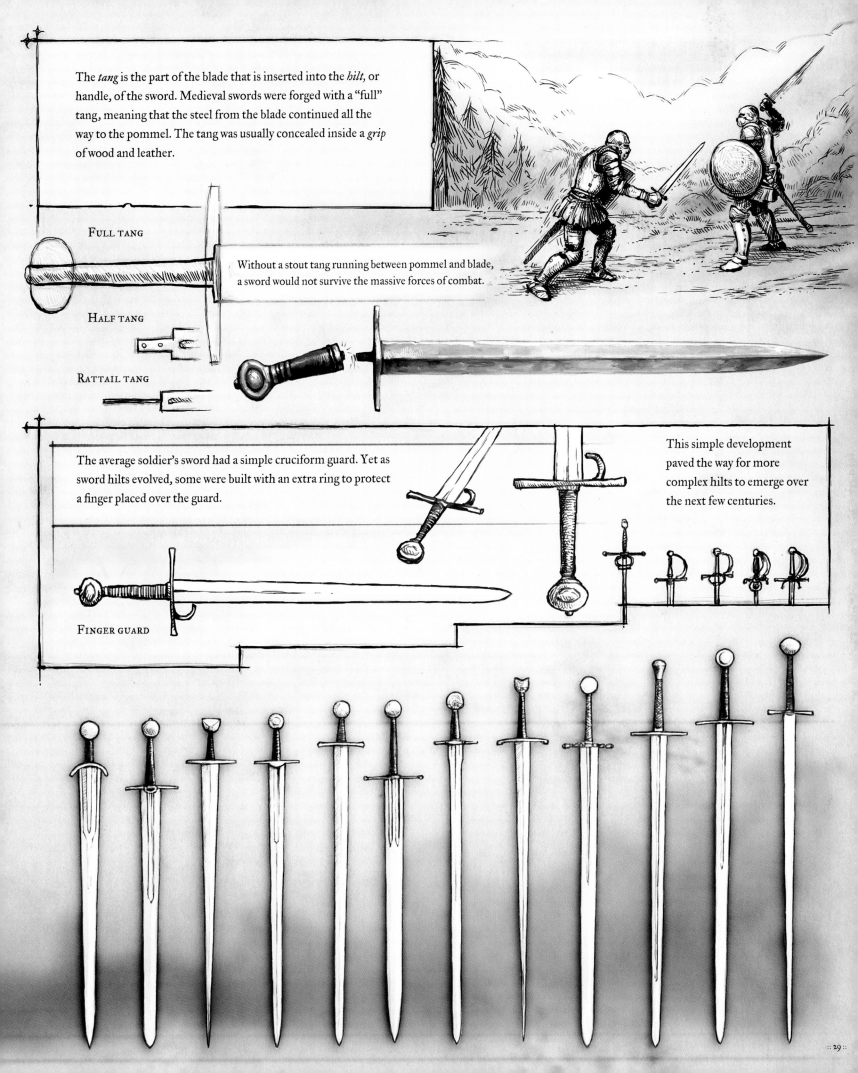

The *tang* is the part of the blade that is inserted into the *hilt*, or handle, of the sword. Medieval swords were forged with a "full" tang, meaning that the steel from the blade continued all the way to the pommel. The tang was usually concealed inside a *grip* of wood and leather.

FULL TANG

Without a stout tang running between pommel and blade, a sword would not survive the massive forces of combat.

HALF TANG

RATTAIL TANG

The average soldier's sword had a simple cruciform guard. Yet as sword hilts evolved, some were built with an extra ring to protect a finger placed over the guard.

This simple development paved the way for more complex hilts to emerge over the next few centuries.

FINGER GUARD

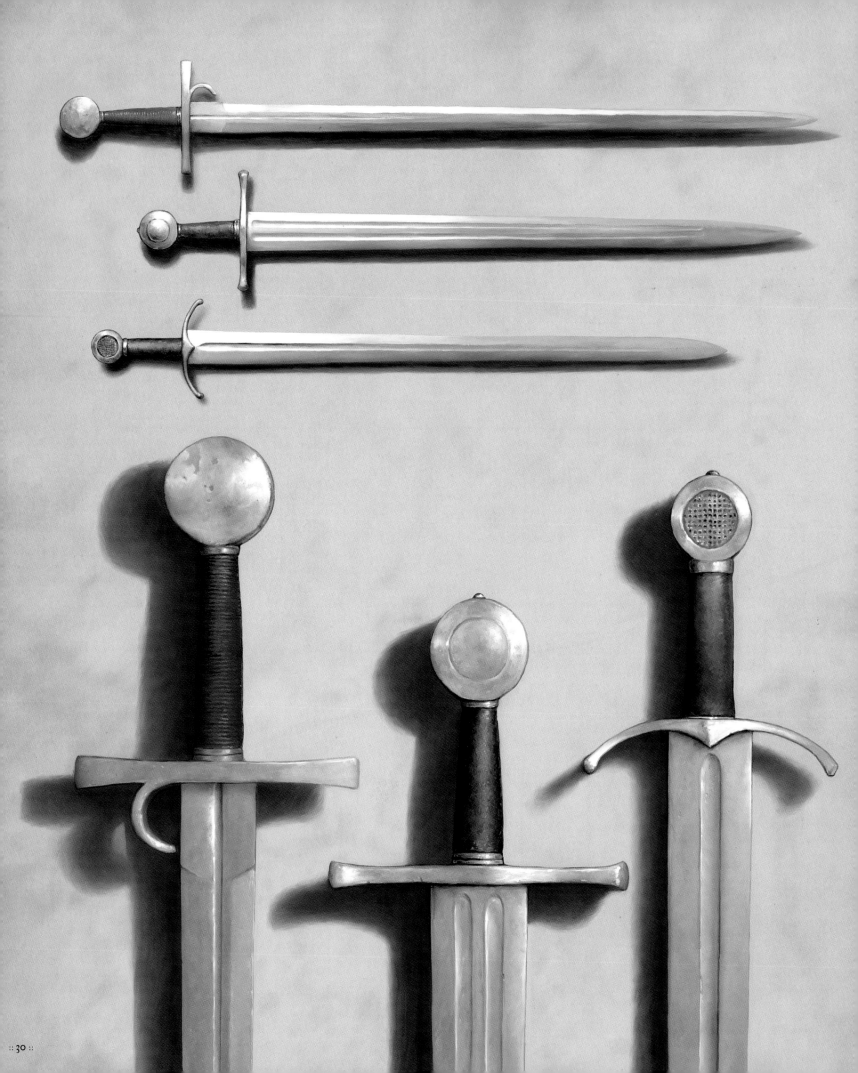

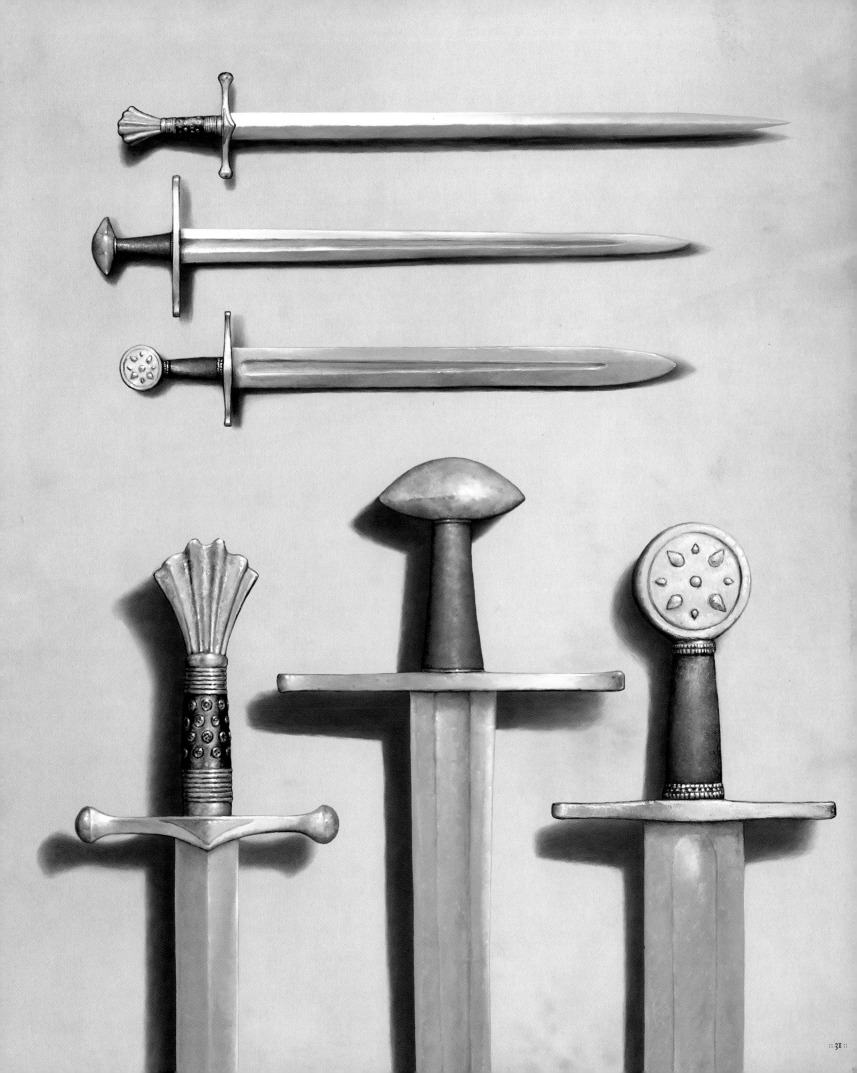

CHAPTER 6

LANDSKNECHTS

The most feared mercenaries of old Europe were known as *landsknechts*. They were highly paid and exceptionally well-trained fighters active in almost every continental war between the late 1400s and the late 1600s. Hailing from such places as Swabia and Bavaria, these soldiers of fortune had a reputation for being elite wielders of the sword.

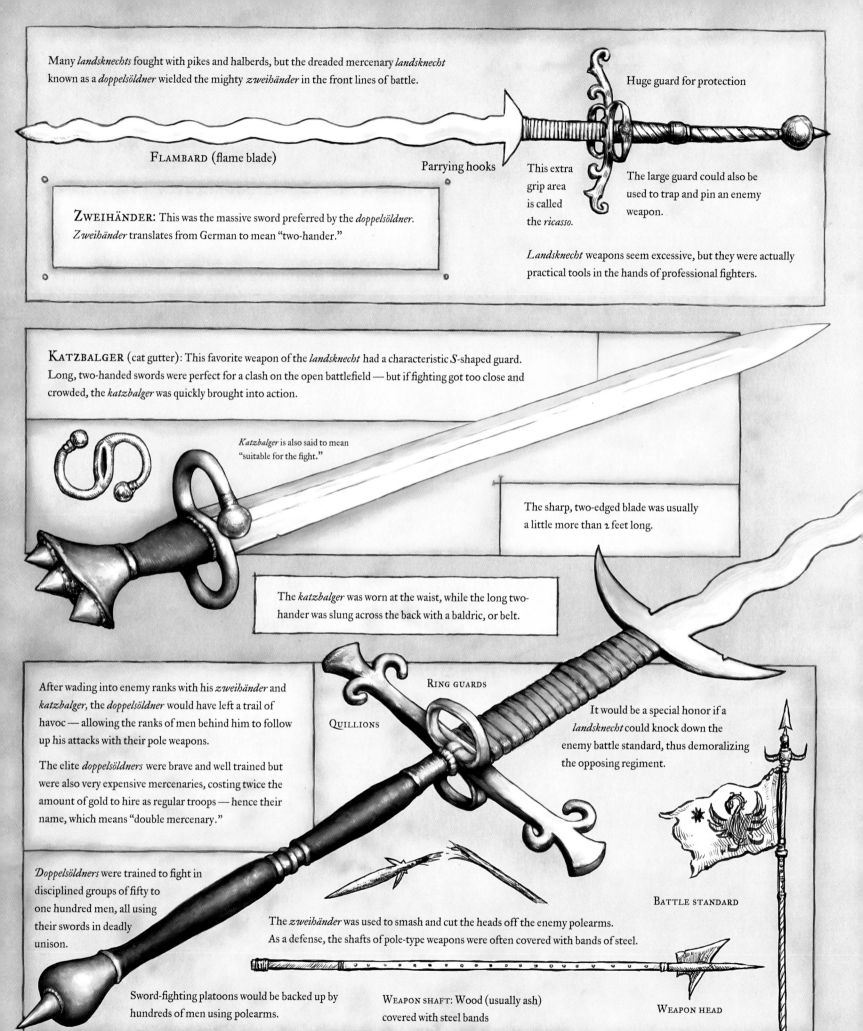

Many *landsknechts* fought with pikes and halberds, but the dreaded mercenary *landsknecht* known as a *doppelsöldner* wielded the mighty *zweihänder* in the front lines of battle.

FLAMBARD (flame blade)

Huge guard for protection

Parrying hooks

This extra grip area is called the *ricasso*.

The large guard could also be used to trap and pin an enemy weapon.

ZWEIHÄNDER: This was the massive sword preferred by the *doppelsöldner*. *Zweihänder* translates from German to mean "two-hander."

Landsknecht weapons seem excessive, but they were actually practical tools in the hands of professional fighters.

KATZBALGER (cat gutter): This favorite weapon of the *landsknecht* had a characteristic *S*-shaped guard. Long, two-handed swords were perfect for a clash on the open battlefield — but if fighting got too close and crowded, the *katzbalger* was quickly brought into action.

Katzbalger is also said to mean "suitable for the fight."

The sharp, two-edged blade was usually a little more than 2 feet long.

The *katzbalger* was worn at the waist, while the long two-hander was slung across the back with a baldric, or belt.

After wading into enemy ranks with his *zweihänder* and *katzbalger*, the *doppelsöldner* would have left a trail of havoc — allowing the ranks of men behind him to follow up his attacks with their pole weapons.

The elite *doppelsöldners* were brave and well trained but were also very expensive mercenaries, costing twice the amount of gold to hire as regular troops — hence their name, which means "double mercenary."

QUILLIONS

RING GUARDS

It would be a special honor if a *landsknecht* could knock down the enemy battle standard, thus demoralizing the opposing regiment.

BATTLE STANDARD

Doppelsöldners were trained to fight in disciplined groups of fifty to one hundred men, all using their swords in deadly unison.

The *zweihänder* was used to smash and cut the heads off the enemy polearms. As a defense, the shafts of pole-type weapons were often covered with bands of steel.

Sword-fighting platoons would be backed up by hundreds of men using polearms.

WEAPON SHAFT: Wood (usually ash) covered with steel bands

WEAPON HEAD

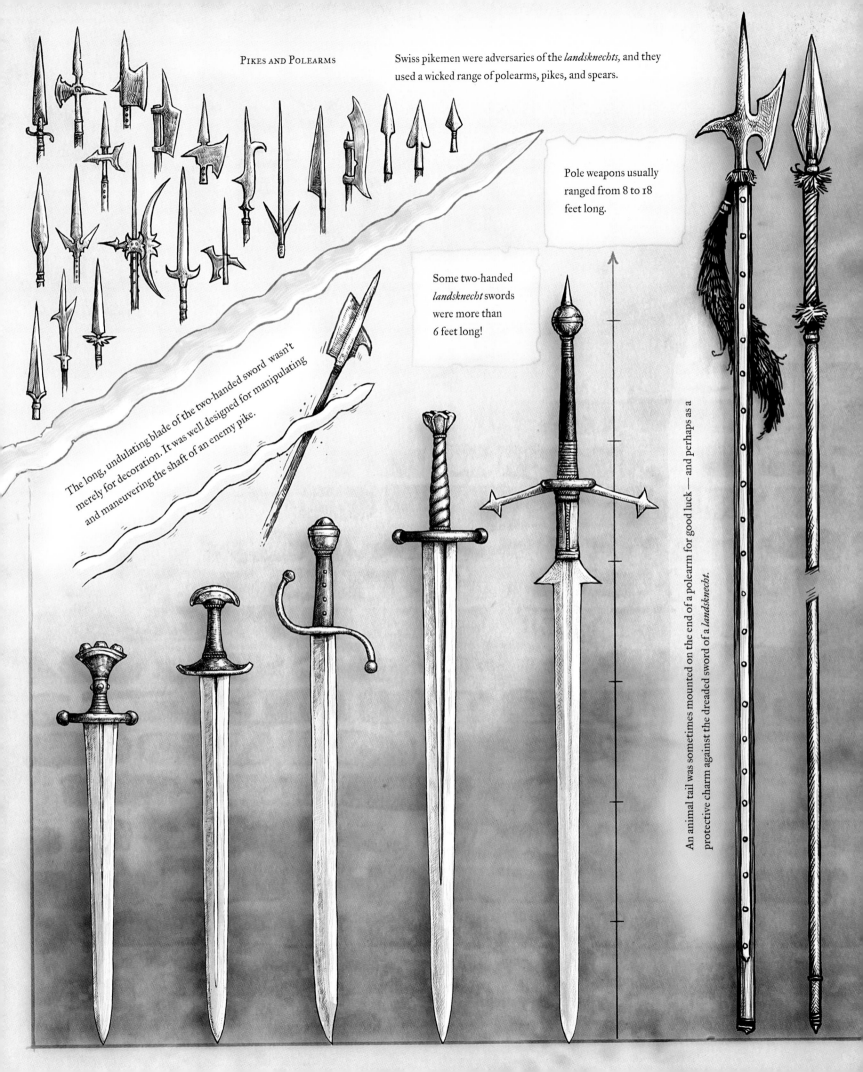

PIKES AND POLEARMS

Swiss pikemen were adversaries of the *landsknechts*, and they used a wicked range of polearms, pikes, and spears.

Pole weapons usually ranged from 8 to 18 feet long.

Some two-handed *landsknecht* swords were more than 6 feet long!

The long, undulating blade of the two-handed sword wasn't merely for decoration. It was well designed for manipulating and maneuvering the shaft of an enemy pike.

An animal tail was sometimes mounted on the end of a polearm for good luck — and perhaps as a protective charm against the dreaded sword of a *landsknecht*.

CHAPTER —7—

Knights

The medieval knight was a dominant force on the battlefield.

Whether on foot or on horseback, the knight had mastered the use of the sword in both conquest and defense.

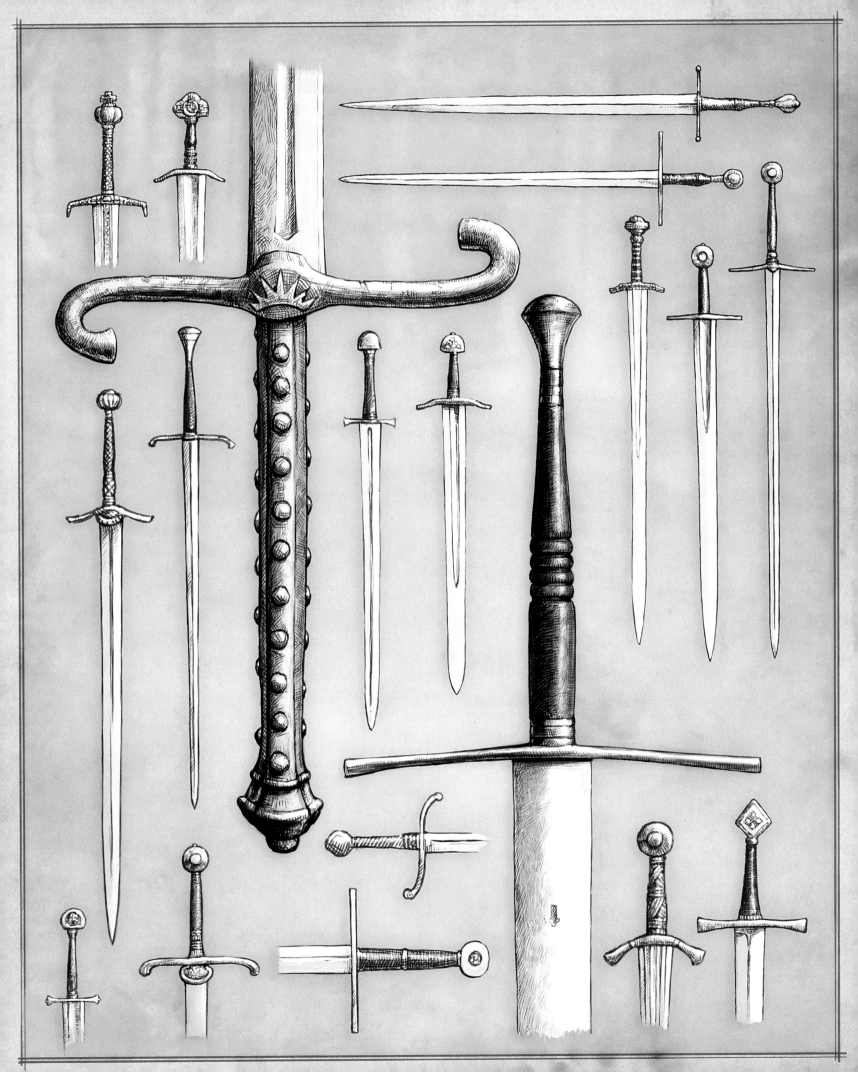

A knight's shield, with coat of arms

A typical sword and shield were essential, but many knights also opted for large, two-handed battle swords in combat.

It was not uncommon to have weapons tethered to armor with a leash of chain. This would make retrieving a dropped weapon possible in the chaos of a fight.

Knights were expected to be chivalrous, despite their lethal training.

ON HORSEBACK

On the battlefield, a mounted knight was like a tank compared to those on foot — at least until pike formations made cavalry charges less practical.

WAR HORSE

BATTLE SWORD

Old manuscripts depict knights battling with brutal, spiky battle swords. From such documents, we can see that the sword was sometimes used like a mace or club.

The stirrup was an incredibly important invention that allowed the knight to stand and fight from a horse's back with excellent balance and leverage.

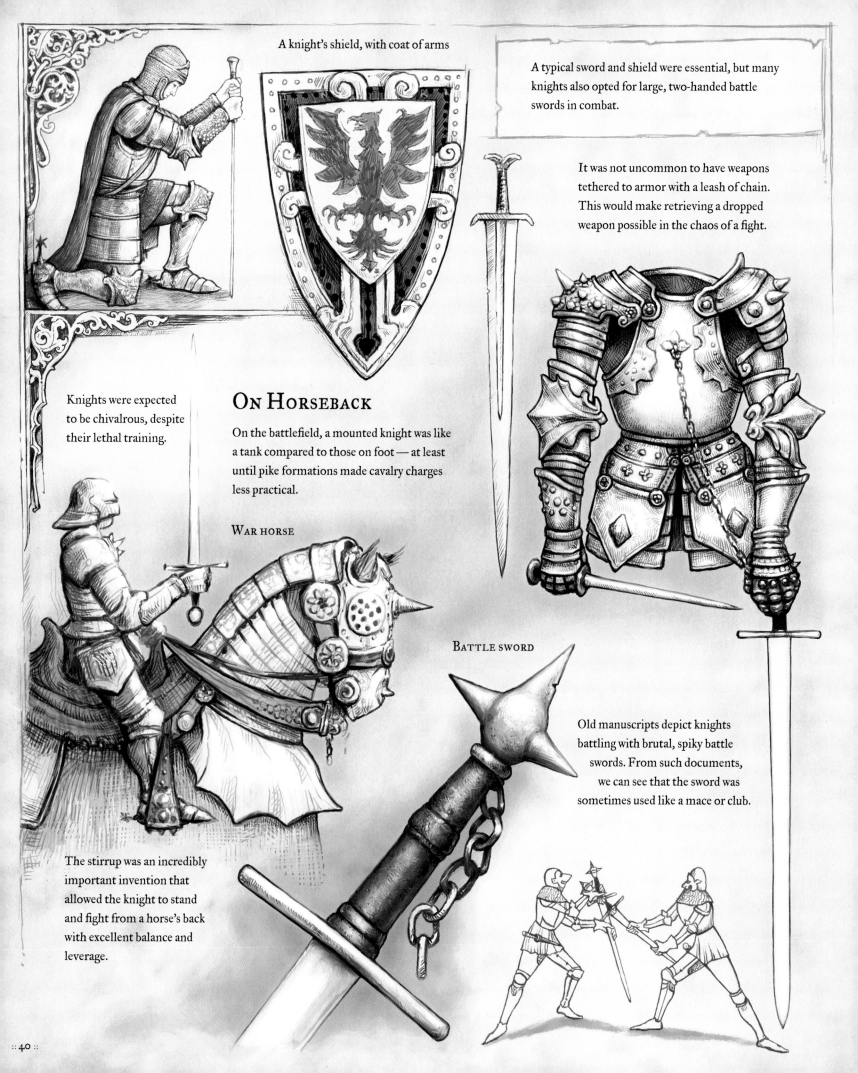

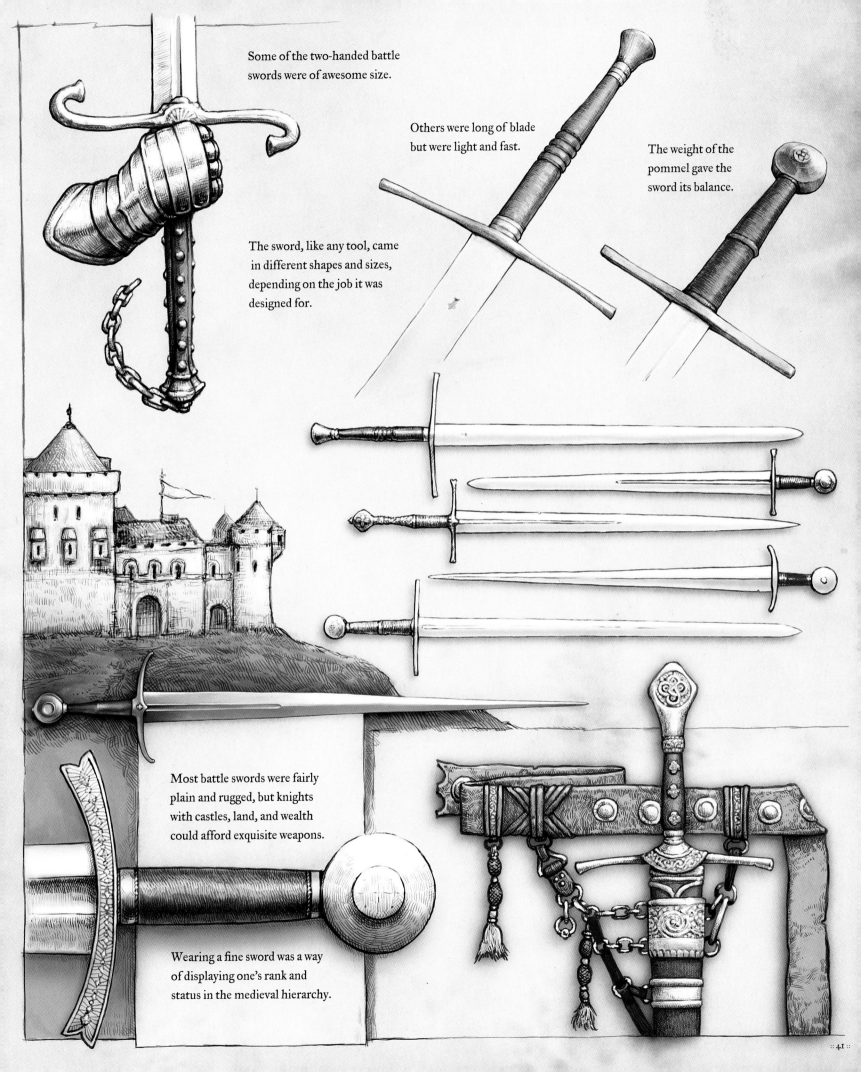

Some of the two-handed battle swords were of awesome size.

Others were long of blade but were light and fast.

The weight of the pommel gave the sword its balance.

The sword, like any tool, came in different shapes and sizes, depending on the job it was designed for.

Most battle swords were fairly plain and rugged, but knights with castles, land, and wealth could afford exquisite weapons.

Wearing a fine sword was a way of displaying one's rank and status in the medieval hierarchy.

CHAPTER 8

KINGS

As the dark ages of mass migration ended, Europe saw the formation of states and the rise of monarchies across its lands. Thus began an age of kings.

The sword was taken up by many a king — sometimes far abroad in conquest or crusade, sometimes at home — as the last defense of a besieged castle. The sword lives on in medieval monuments and songs as proof that it was the defining weapon of this era.

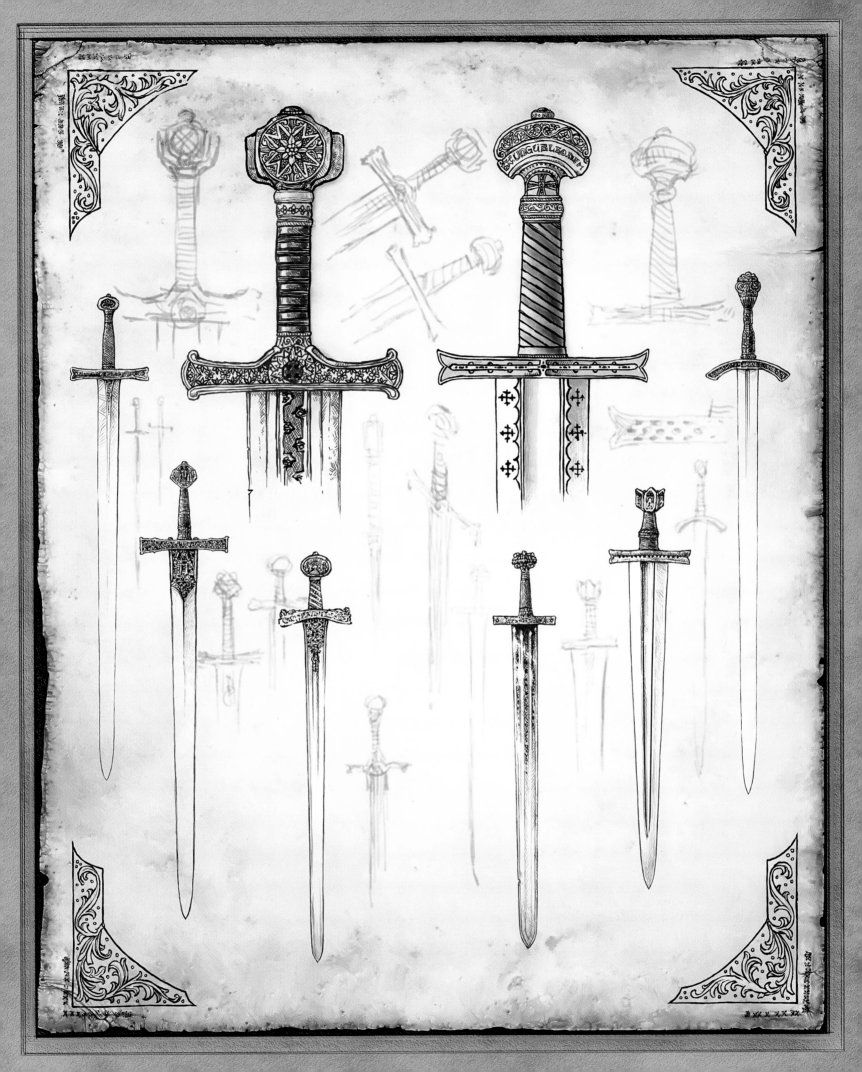

If a king did not inherit a royal sword from his ancestors, he might, if he was rich enough, commission a sword to be newly crafted.

A masterpiece could cost a small fortune.

In ancient times, a small handful of master sword-smiths held the secrets to forging battle-worthy blades. They kept their secrets close, which made their swords all the more precious.

A blade crafted by a master was thought to have its own spirit and would often be given a name. It was handled with respect like an heirloom —

a treasure fit for a king.

A monarch was thought to wield divine authority with his sword. The sword, rather than the scepter, was the true symbol of power.

A king used the mere touch of his sword to dub a man "Sir Knight."

Kissing the blade of a king's sword was done to give a most solemn oath.

Almost anywhere a king went, he went armed. In fact, a sword usually accompanied a king from his coronation all the way to his tomb.

The sword of a king was a powerful symbol, but above all, it was a deadly weapon for the battlefield.

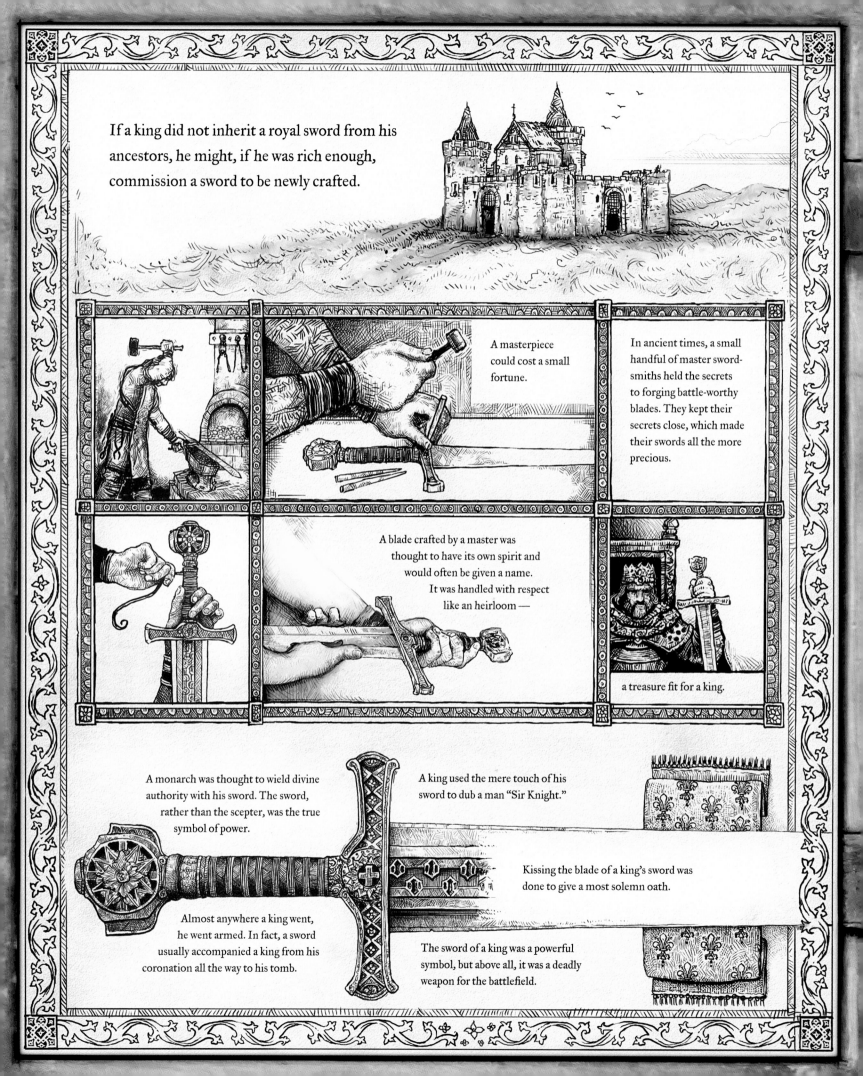

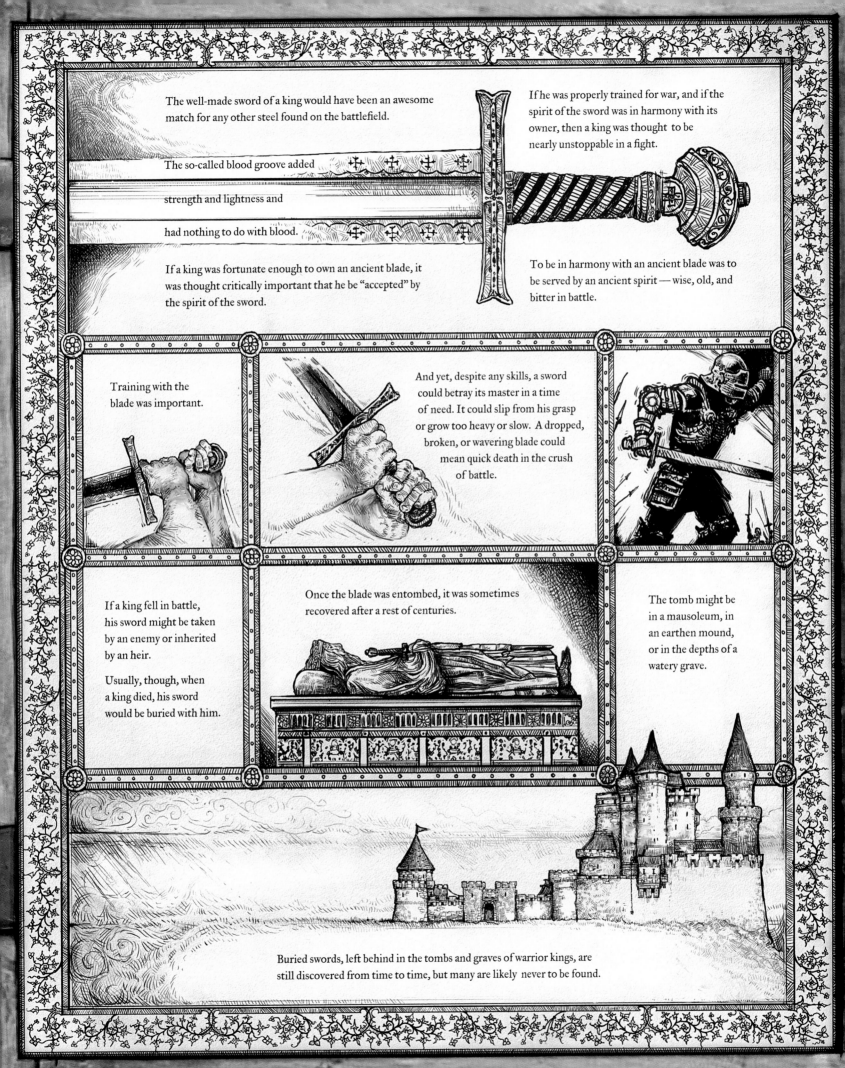

The well-made sword of a king would have been an awesome match for any other steel found on the battlefield.

If he was properly trained for war, and if the spirit of the sword was in harmony with its owner, then a king was thought to be nearly unstoppable in a fight.

The so-called blood groove added

strength and lightness and

had nothing to do with blood.

If a king was fortunate enough to own an ancient blade, it was thought critically important that he be "accepted" by the spirit of the sword.

To be in harmony with an ancient blade was to be served by an ancient spirit — wise, old, and bitter in battle.

Training with the blade was important.

And yet, despite any skills, a sword could betray its master in a time of need. It could slip from his grasp or grow too heavy or slow. A dropped, broken, or wavering blade could mean quick death in the crush of battle.

If a king fell in battle, his sword might be taken by an enemy or inherited by an heir.

Usually, though, when a king died, his sword would be buried with him.

Once the blade was entombed, it was sometimes recovered after a rest of centuries.

The tomb might be in a mausoleum, in an earthen mound, or in the depths of a watery grave.

Buried swords, left behind in the tombs and graves of warrior kings, are still discovered from time to time, but many are likely never to be found.

CHAPTER 9

SAMURAI

To be a samurai was to be a man of the sword. The sword was not merely a weapon of choice; it was essential — one could not be a samurai without it. In fact, the samurai warrior and his sword were almost never separated. Though the samurai might leave his larger weapons out of doors, he kept a short sword near at hand at all times. Such was the way of the samurai.

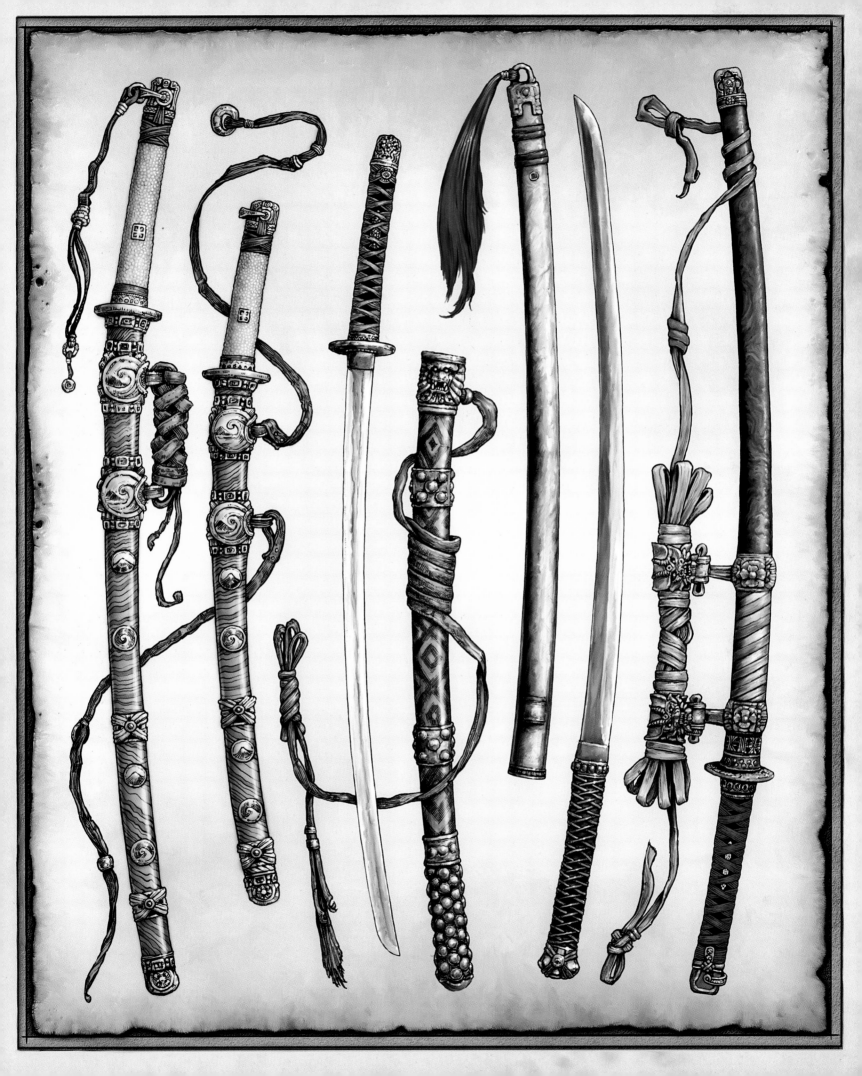

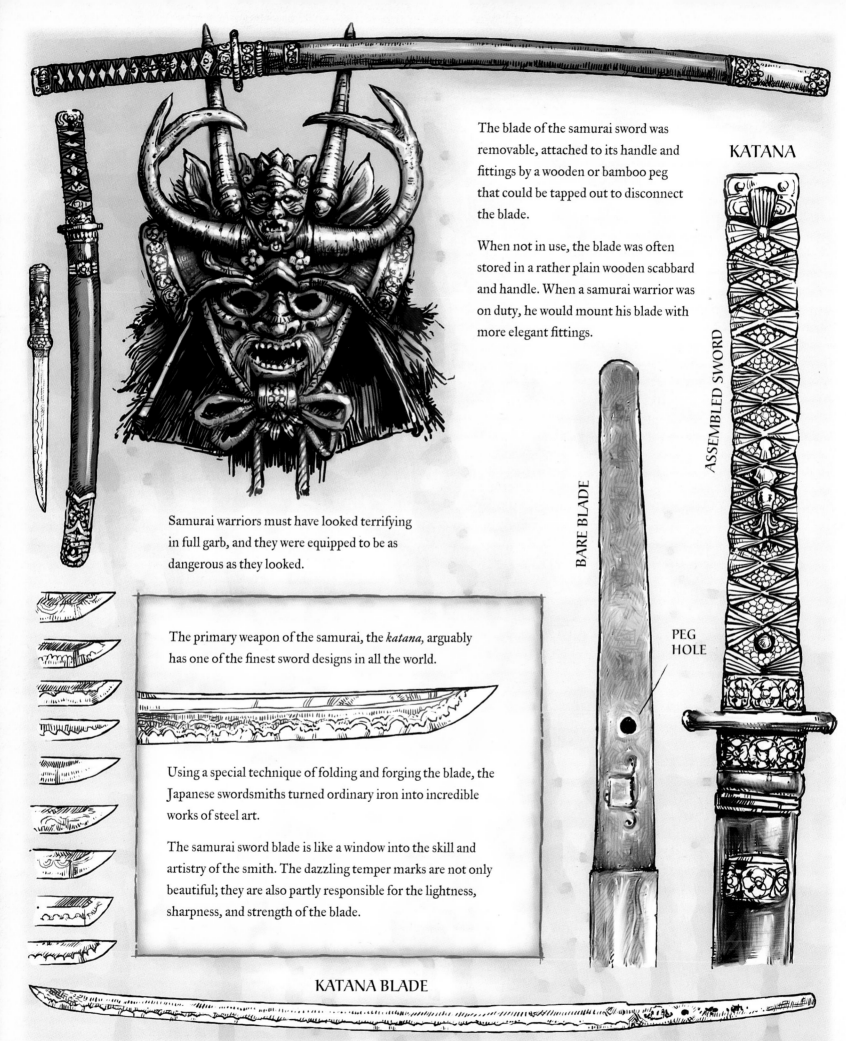

The blade of the samurai sword was removable, attached to its handle and fittings by a wooden or bamboo peg that could be tapped out to disconnect the blade.

When not in use, the blade was often stored in a rather plain wooden scabbard and handle. When a samurai warrior was on duty, he would mount his blade with more elegant fittings.

KATANA

ASSEMBLED SWORD

BARE BLADE

PEG HOLE

Samurai warriors must have looked terrifying in full garb, and they were equipped to be as dangerous as they looked.

The primary weapon of the samurai, the *katana*, arguably has one of the finest sword designs in all the world.

Using a special technique of folding and forging the blade, the Japanese swordsmiths turned ordinary iron into incredible works of steel art.

The samurai sword blade is like a window into the skill and artistry of the smith. The dazzling temper marks are not only beautiful; they are also partly responsible for the lightness, sharpness, and strength of the blade.

KATANA BLADE

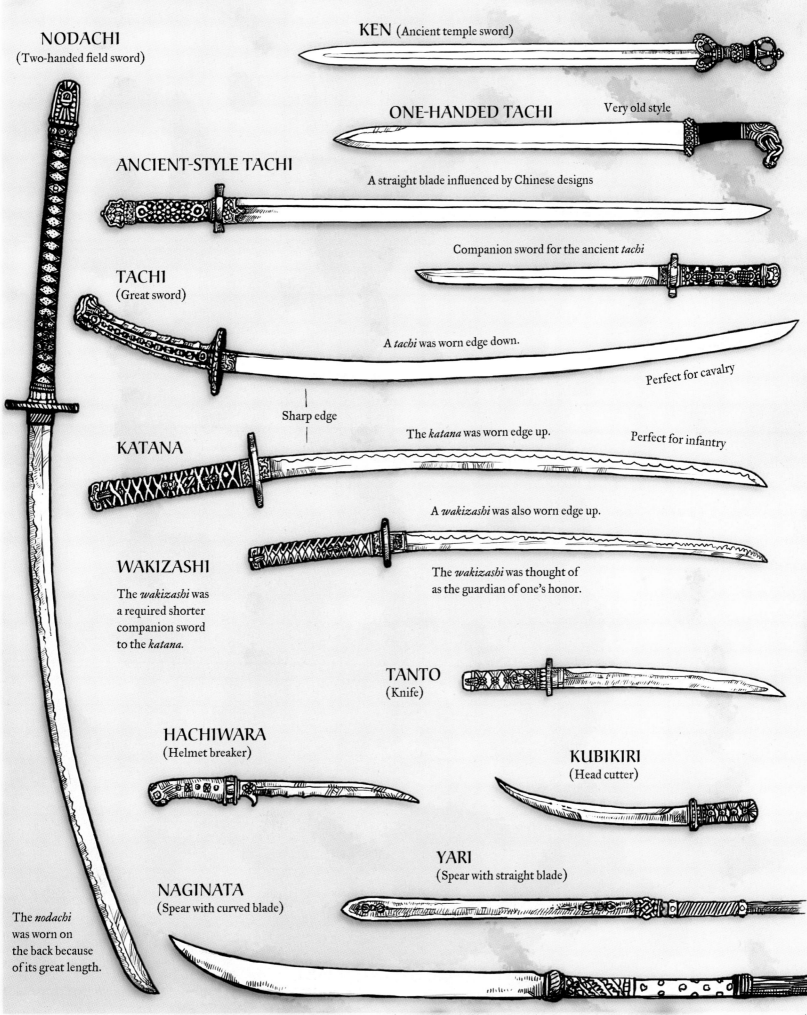

NODACHI
(Two-handed field sword)

KEN (Ancient temple sword)

ONE-HANDED TACHI   Very old style

ANCIENT-STYLE TACHI

A straight blade influenced by Chinese designs

TACHI
(Great sword)

Companion sword for the ancient *tachi*

A *tachi* was worn edge down.

Perfect for cavalry

Sharp edge

KATANA   The *katana* was worn edge up.   Perfect for infantry

WAKIZASHI   A *wakizashi* was also worn edge up.

The *wakizashi* was
a required shorter
companion sword
to the *katana*.

The *wakizashi* was thought of
as the guardian of one's honor.

TANTO
(Knife)

HACHIWARA
(Helmet breaker)

KUBIKIRI
(Head cutter)

YARI
(Spear with straight blade)

NAGINATA
(Spear with curved blade)

The *nodachi*
was worn on
the back because
of its great length.

CHAPTER 10

NINJA

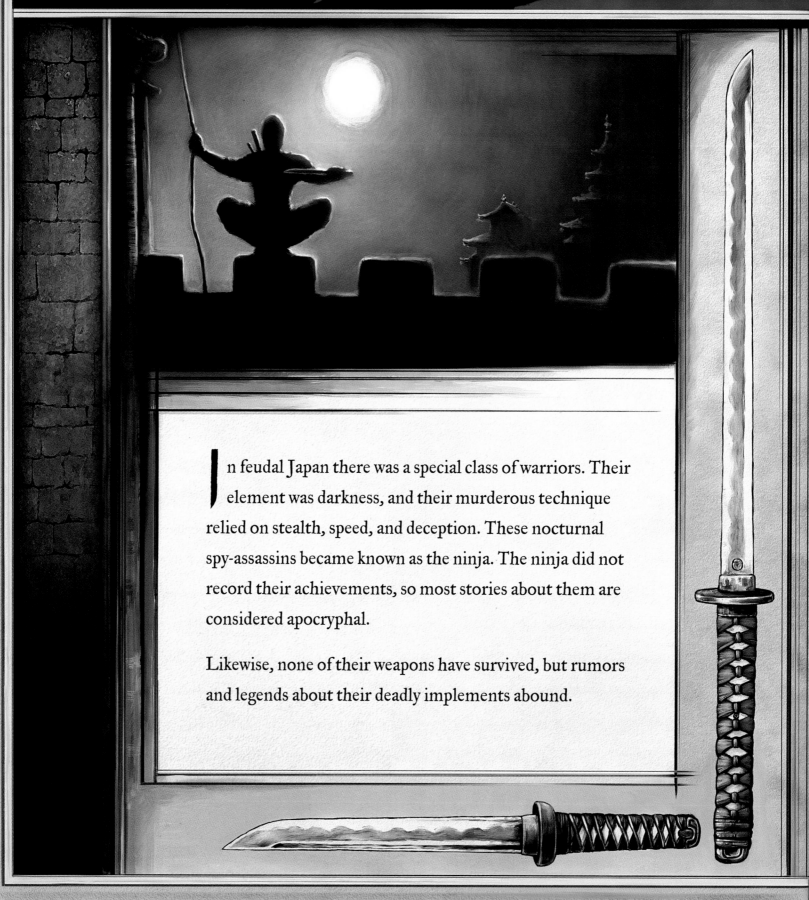

In feudal Japan there was a special class of warriors. Their element was darkness, and their murderous technique relied on stealth, speed, and deception. These nocturnal spy-assassins became known as the ninja. The ninja did not record their achievements, so most stories about them are considered apocryphal.

Likewise, none of their weapons have survived, but rumors and legends about their deadly implements abound.

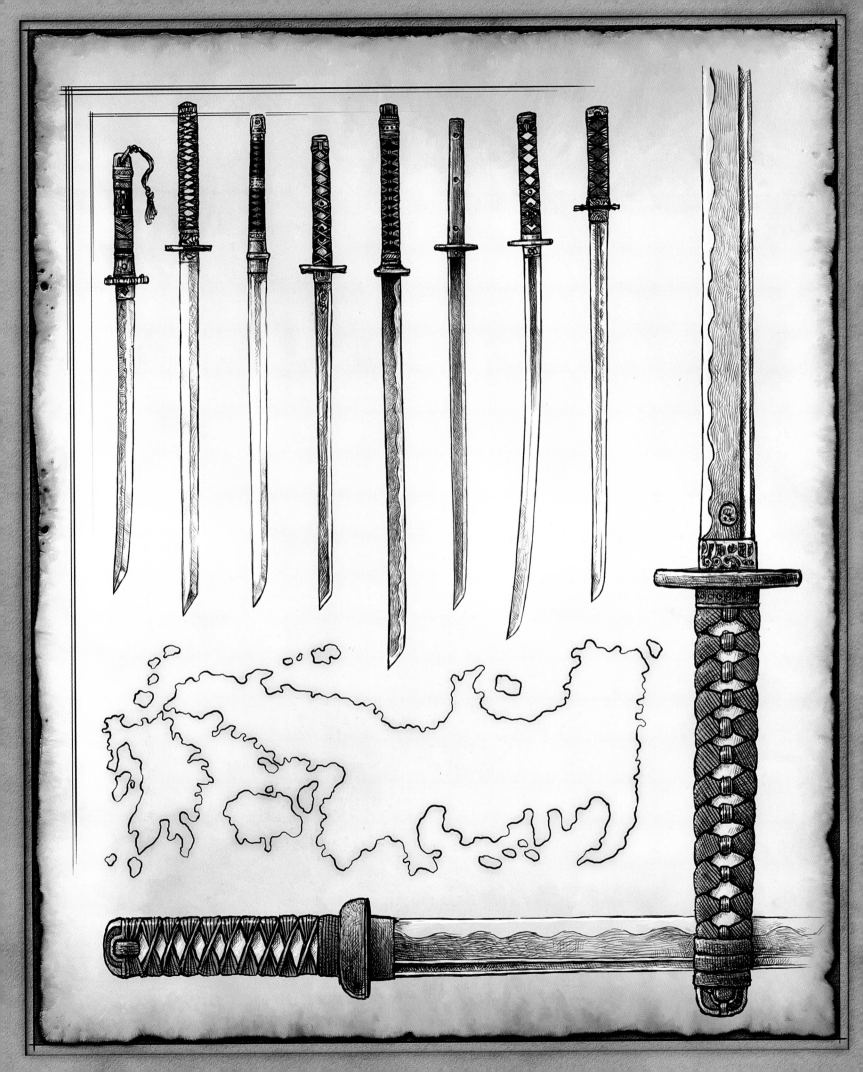

KUSARI-FUNDO

A weapon devised by the ninja consisting of two weights (*fundo*) connected by a chain, which allowed for throwing and swinging attacks. With the proper technique, the *kusari-fundo* could also be used to trap an opponent's arms, legs, or weapons. Blades may also have sometimes been attached to the weights.

Many ninja weapons employed cords and tethers. Some tethers were made from women's hair or horsehair; others were made of silk, leather, or chain.

KYOKETSU-SHOGE

A hooked, knife-like weapon usually connected to a long cord or chain. Excellent for keeping one's distance from one's opponent.

Every part of the *shoge* had a functional use, whether for attack, defense, or infiltration.

KAGINAWA

A long cord with a hook or blade at the end seems to have been a regular part of the ninja arsenal. Like the *shuriken*, it was probably used to create an opening for a sword attack.

Corded and tethered weapons could be employed in a throw-and-retrieve action. Cords and tethers could also be used in conjunction with a number of binding techniques to tie an enemy's arms or legs with a flick of the wrist.

SHURIKEN

Small knives or darts, used by the ninja to distract or wound an enemy. They were easily concealed on the body and could be brought into use at a moment's notice.

HIMOGATANA

A steel stiletto that was easily drawn for a fast attack.

Hidden weapons on a ninja's arm

Deadly little implements, *shuriken* could be used at close range or at a medium distance. A surprise *shuriken* attack could facilitate an escape or could be used to close the gap with a foe, allowing for a deadly follow-up attack.

Chains were light and strong and would have resisted cutting or breaking, but cords and ropes would be quieter, perfect for stealthy nocturnal attacks.

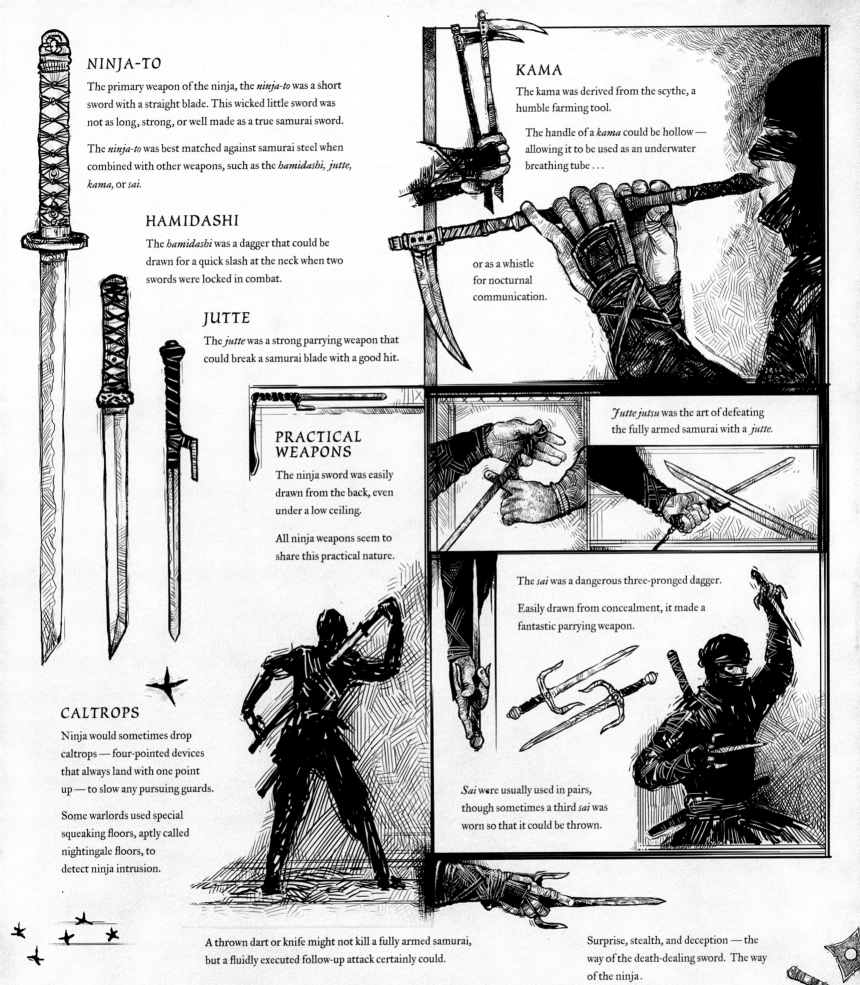

NINJA-TO

The primary weapon of the ninja, the *ninja-to* was a short sword with a straight blade. This wicked little sword was not as long, strong, or well made as a true samurai sword.

The *ninja-to* was best matched against samurai steel when combined with other weapons, such as the *hamidashi*, *jutte*, *kama*, or *sai*.

HAMIDASHI

The *hamidashi* was a dagger that could be drawn for a quick slash at the neck when two swords were locked in combat.

JUTTE

The *jutte* was a strong parrying weapon that could break a samurai blade with a good hit.

PRACTICAL WEAPONS

The ninja sword was easily drawn from the back, even under a low ceiling.

All ninja weapons seem to share this practical nature.

CALTROPS

Ninja would sometimes drop caltrops — four-pointed devices that always land with one point up — to slow any pursuing guards.

Some warlords used special squeaking floors, aptly called nightingale floors, to detect ninja intrusion.

KAMA

The kama was derived from the scythe, a humble farming tool.

The handle of a *kama* could be hollow — allowing it to be used as an underwater breathing tube . . .

or as a whistle for nocturnal communication.

Jutte jutsu was the art of defeating the fully armed samurai with a *jutte*.

The *sai* was a dangerous three-pronged dagger.

Easily drawn from concealment, it made a fantastic parrying weapon.

Sai were usually used in pairs, though sometimes a third *sai* was worn so that it could be thrown.

A thrown dart or knife might not kill a fully armed samurai, but a fluidly executed follow-up attack certainly could.

Surprise, stealth, and deception — the way of the death-dealing sword. The way of the ninja.

SILLA KNIGHTS

One thousand years ago in the Silla Kingdom, now Korea, a martial art was developed that was married to a code of ethics and the pursuit of honor. The young knights who swore to this code spent the flower of their youth training — often in the forests and mountains. These bold students of the sword were known as the knights of Silla.

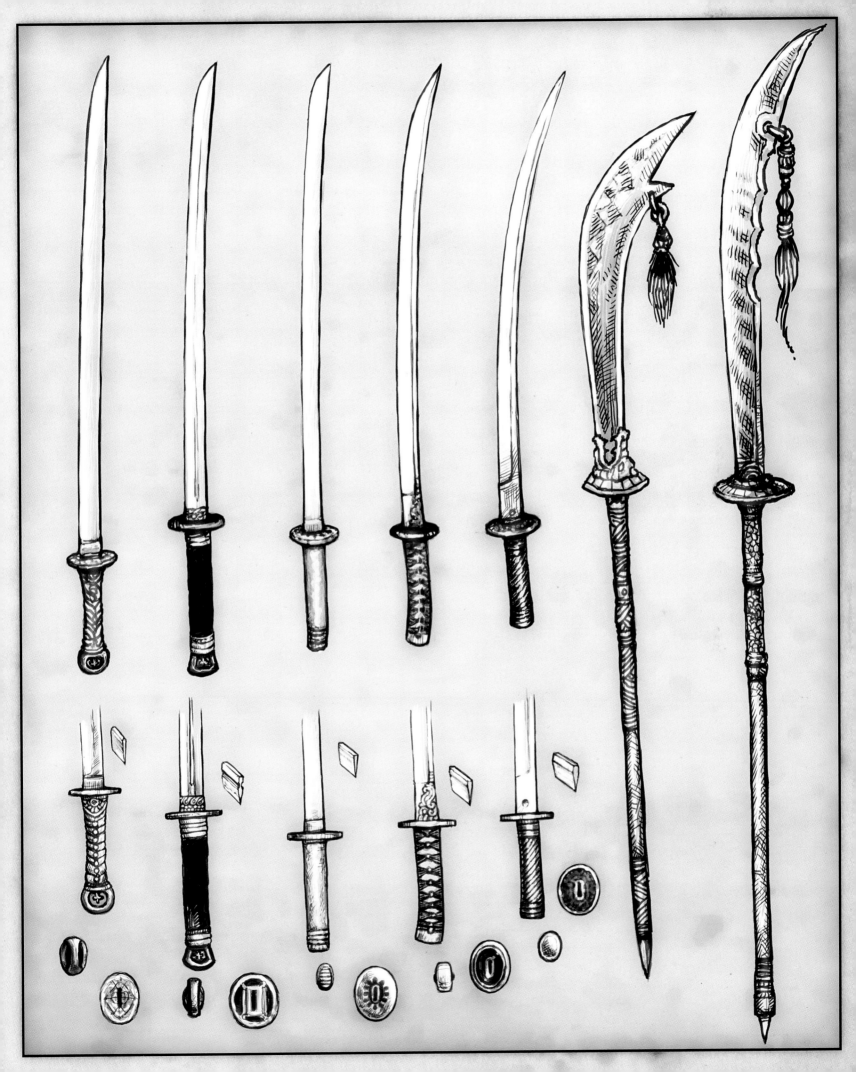

Gumdo, the Way of the Sword

Silla knights sojourned into the wild, alone or in groups, to train and study.

When they returned from their wanderings, the Silla knights contributed to many a crucial battle.

The Silla warrior sought to be in harmony with the forces of nature.

Silla fighting styles are described in the few remaining ancient Korean texts:

Twin-sword style

Shield with sword

Spear sword

Crescent sword

Twin swords on horseback

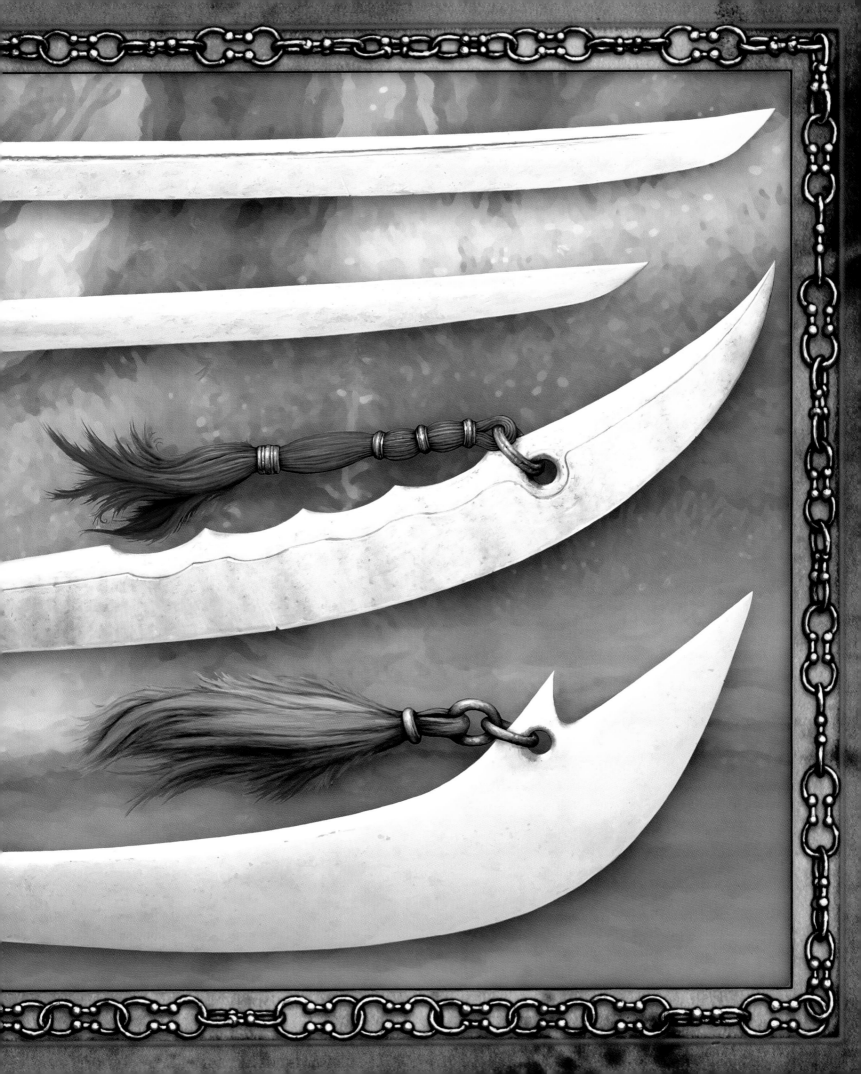

CHAPTER +12+ EASTERN MASTERS

The kingdoms and territories of China have seen numerous powerful dynasties over thousands of years. According to Chinese tradition, the sword is sacred, and its mastery is a virtue of the highest order.

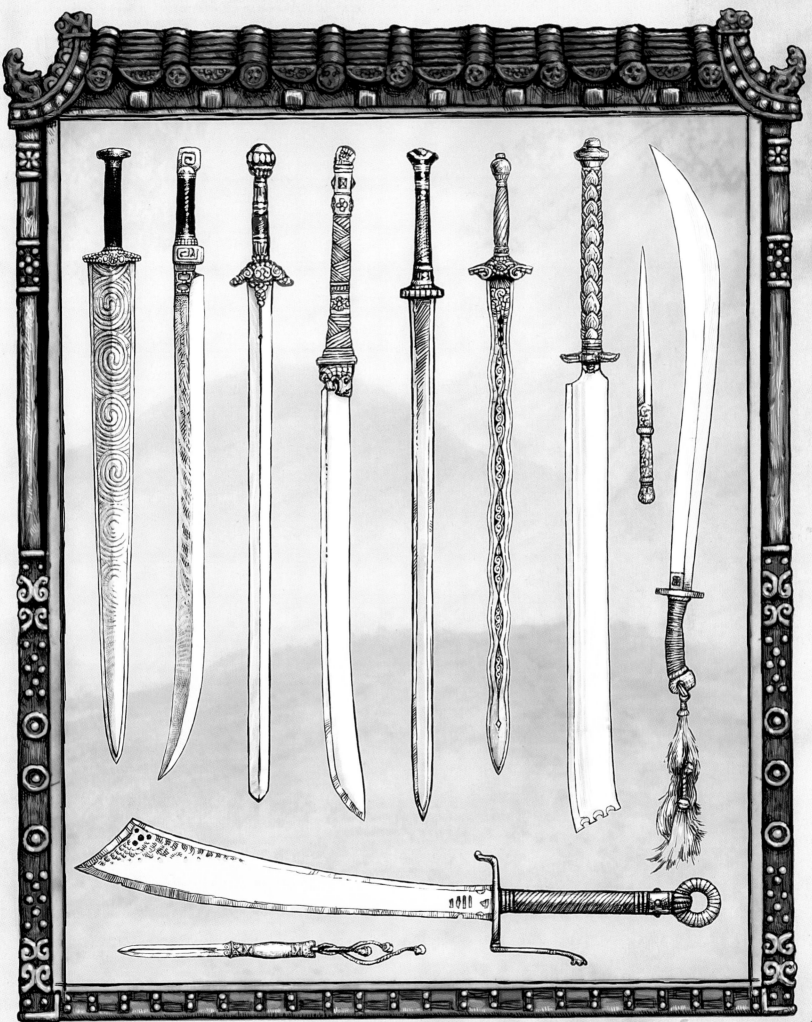

Blade craft in ancient China actually started with swords carved from stone. As metallurgy advanced, blades were forged from bronze, copper, and other easily worked metals.

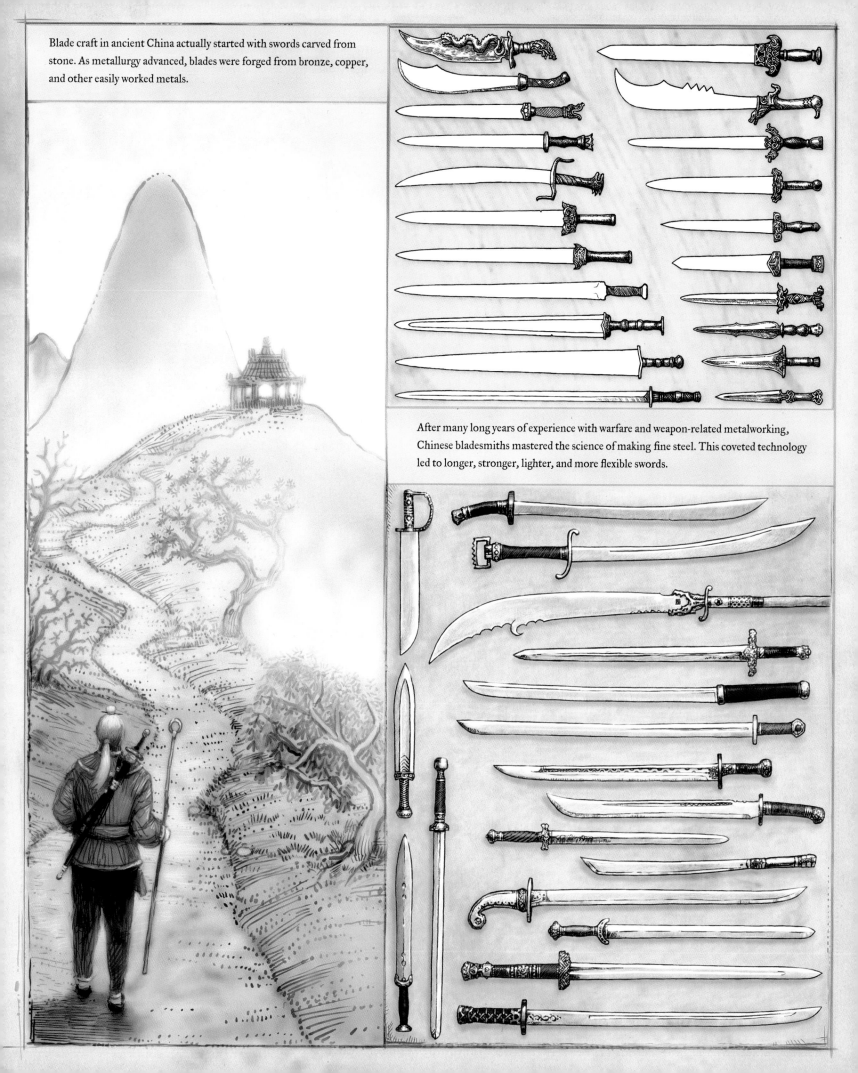

After many long years of experience with warfare and weapon-related metalworking, Chinese bladesmiths mastered the science of making fine steel. This coveted technology led to longer, stronger, lighter, and more flexible swords.

JIAN: A two-edged style of sword that is the culmination of three thousand years of Chinese sword making.

"One who wields a sword reveals his emptiness to his opponent, gives him an advantageous opening, makes his move after him, and arrives before he does."

— Philosopher Zhuangzi, *Discoursing on Swords*

Mastering the *jian* was said to require a perfect combination of mind, spirit, and life force.

Mind: *Yi*

Spirit: *Shen*

Life force: *Qi*

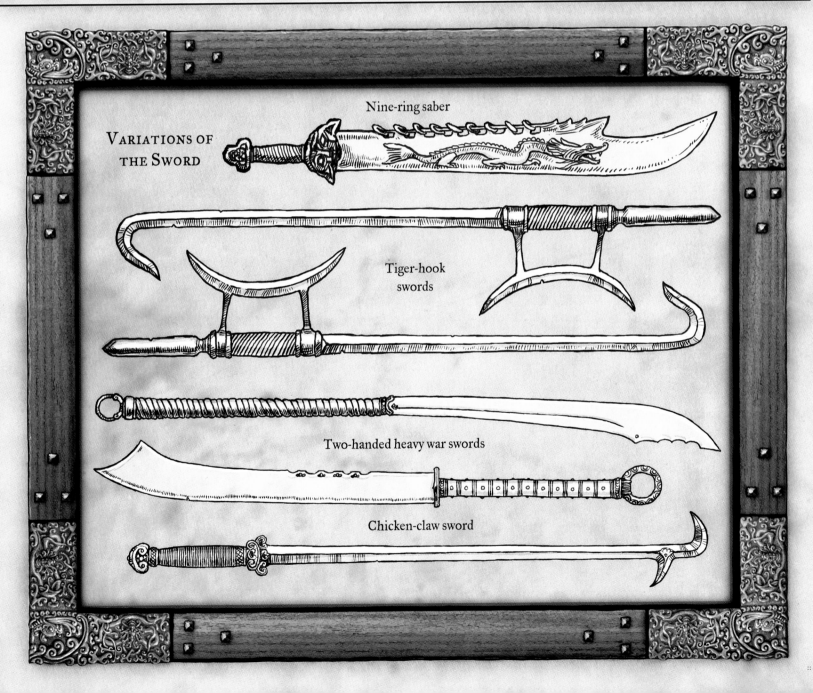

VARIATIONS OF THE SWORD

Nine-ring saber

Tiger-hook swords

Two-handed heavy war swords

Chicken-claw sword

CHAPTER 13

WAR CHIEFS

Scattered across the harsh and untamed lands of this earth, fierce and determined people have battled for existence since prehistoric times. A nearly universal role has emerged for the bravest and wisest of any people — that of the war chief. These leaders of the warrior class have guided their people through good times and bad, starvation and plenty, chaos and stability. The sword is a tool and symbol of the war chief, be it raised against invasion or worn proudly in times of peace.

Central African Salampasu sword

THROWING SWORDS

Some swords were designed for throwing. They would require a proper balance to fly true, as well as at least one cruelly hooked blade to strike down the intended target.

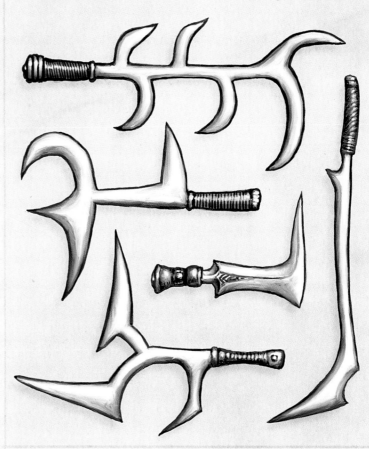

THE MASK OF A SALAMPASU WAR CHIEF

East of the Kasai River, in the Congo region of Africa, live a people known as the Salampasu, who were once fierce warriors. They were described as terrifying by neighboring peoples because of their frightening masks and the eager swords they brought to battle. Three castes in this culture were distinguished by the three styles of masks: the hunters, the warriors, and, above all, the mighty and merciless war chief of the tribe.

In most cultures, the primary purposes of the sword are for fighting in war and for use in self-defense. Another purpose of the sword is to act as a tool for the harvest or the hunt. It is also used to keep order, to maintain justice, and in some cases, to perform executions. Many warriors consider themselves naked when they are without this noble weapon. This is especially true of the war chief, since the sword is a potent symbol of his power and dominance.

Whether a sword is built for actual combat or not, it is often crafted as a beautiful work of art. The style, form, and decoration can reflect much about the culture of the people who made the sword. Each nuance of design is rarely random and is likely very significant. In many corners of the world, the sword is considered a sacred object — a tool of life and death, with great talismanic power.

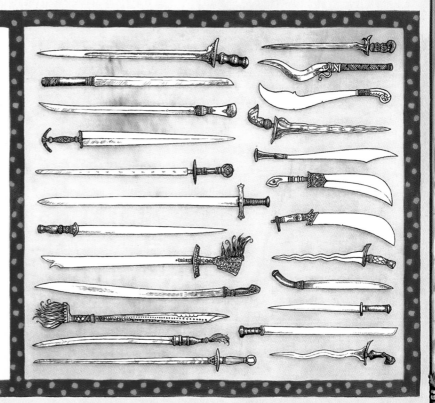

Long-handled tebutje

BLADES OF TEETH

Polynesians, Maori, and other island peoples sometimes affixed the teeth of sharks to wooden handles to make edged weapons called *tebutje*. The bill of a sawfish was also used as an improvised sword.

Short-handled tebutje

Saber-like tebutje

Shark tooth

Sawfish bill

Sawfish-bill sword

THE EVER-PRESENT SWORD

Wherever there is a battle for survival or a struggle for existence, the sword is nearly always present. It has manifested itself in even the remotest and most exotic locations.

BLADES OF STONE

People in the ancient Americas worked pieces of volcanic glass called obsidian into scalpel-sharp weapon blades. Spanish explorers were unhappy to find that these weapons, called *macahuitl,* could strike the head off a horse!

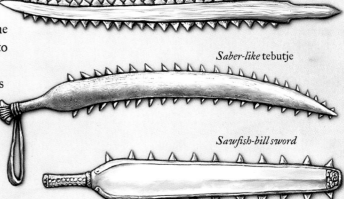
Light macahuitl

Heavy macahuitl

BLADES OF METAL

Weapons edged with teeth or stone could be razor-sharp, but a metal sword was prized for its durability in a fight.

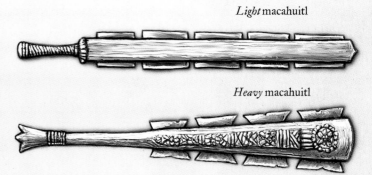

Central African Kuba knife

Moro sword (Philippines)

Double-pointed Upper Congo knife

Crescent-ended Upper Congo knife

Horn-hilted short sword

Khyber long knife

Bornean sword

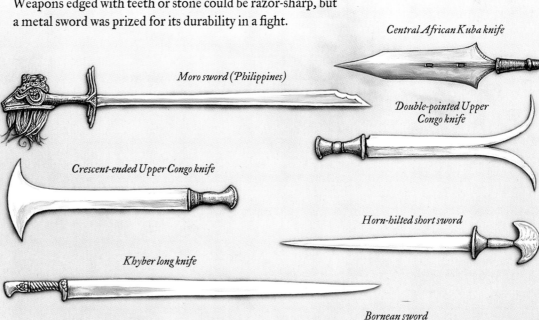

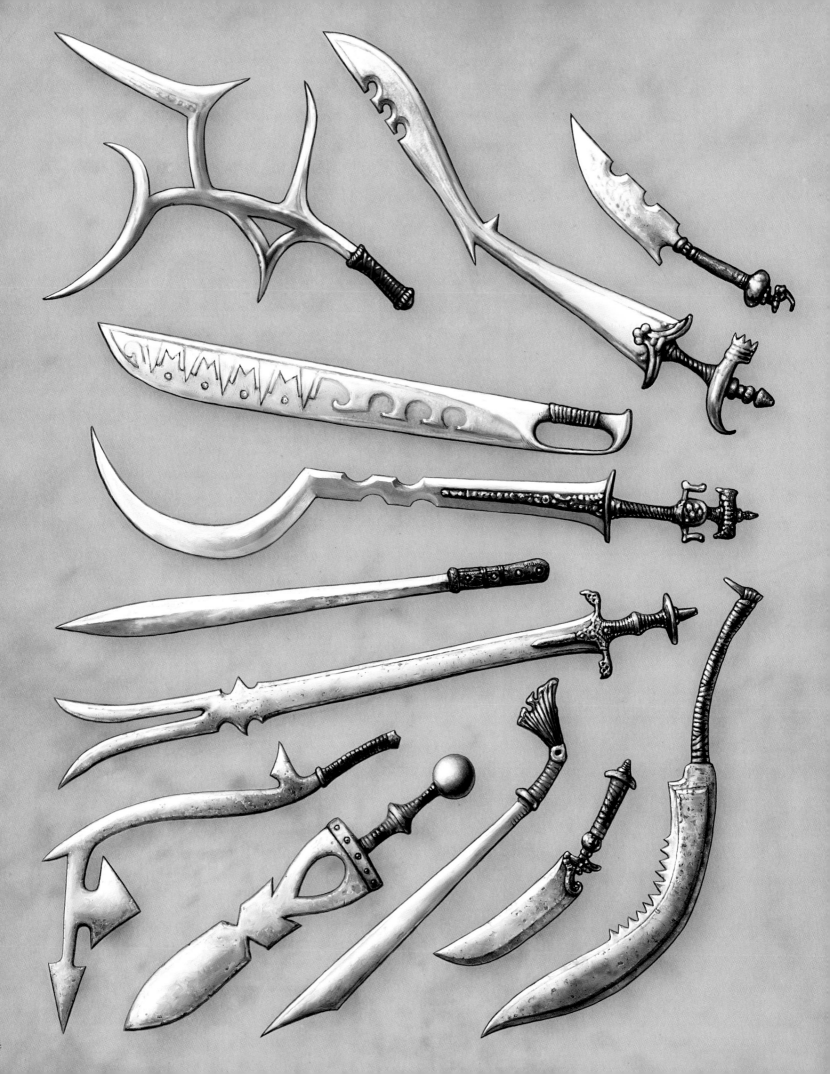

The word *sultan* is Islamic in origin, meaning "power" or "authority." Later, it came to designate a ruler. The first known sultan was Mahmud of Ghazni (998–1030). Sultans often had great fortunes and mighty armies at their command. Fittingly, their weapons were wrought of the finest metals and precious stones.

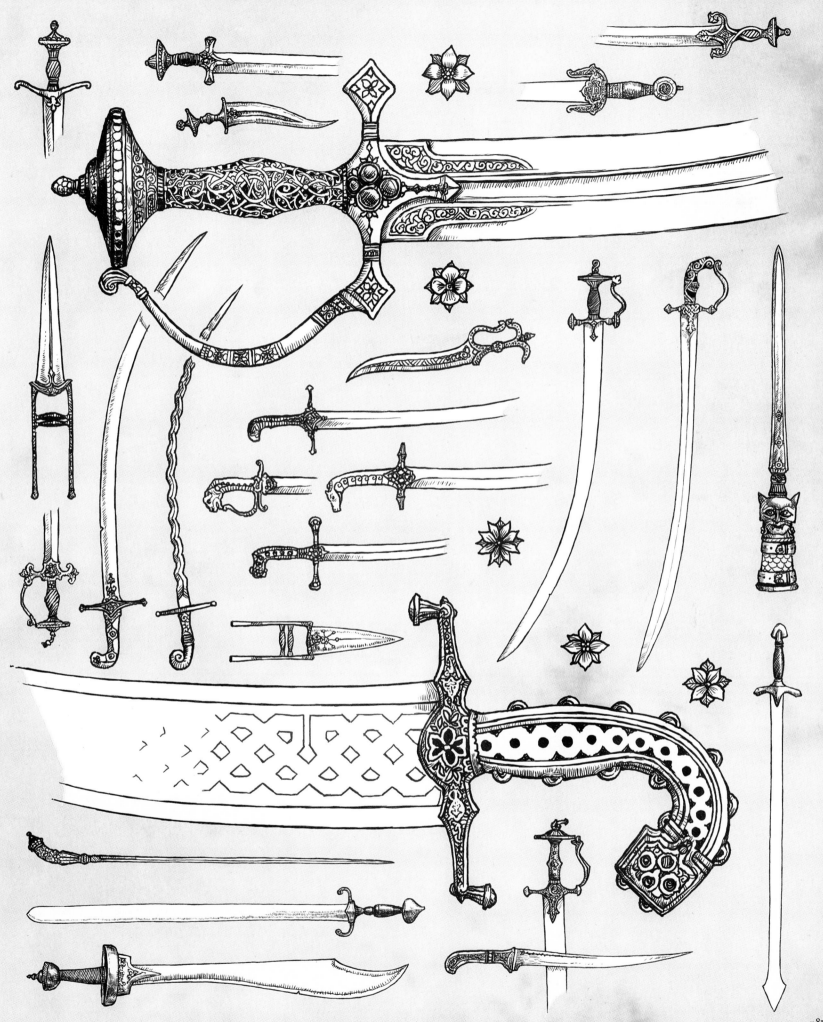

SCIMITARS

A scimitar is a sword with a curved, saber-like blade,
generally from western Asia or the Middle East.

SHAMSHIR

The curved blade of a *shamshir*
was used to slash, rather
than stab, an enemy.

A Persian sultan

The sultans of Persia favored a
thin sword called a *shamshir*.

KILIJ

This wide section of the blade near the
tip is called a *yelman*. Its purpose
was to give the sword a more
devastating chop.

A Turkish sultan

The Ottoman sultans of Turkey
preferred a sword known as the *kilij*.

TALWAR

The *talwar* combines some
of the best features
of a *shamshir*
and a *kilij*.

An Indian sultan

The *talwar* was the sword of choice
for the sultans of medieval India.

DAMASCUS STEEL

Damascus steel is a near-legendary metal that was used by the best sword makers
of the Middle East. It was forged in such a way, by the secret science of its day, to
give it incredible strength and beauty.

Damascene steel, sometimes called watered steel, is an alloy that allows for incredible sharpness.
Blades of this steel were said to be sharp enough to slice effortlessly though a falling piece of silk cloth.
Rumors even spread to medieval Europe about Damascus swords that could chop through other
sword blades without losing their razor-sharp edge, though this was surely an exaggeration.

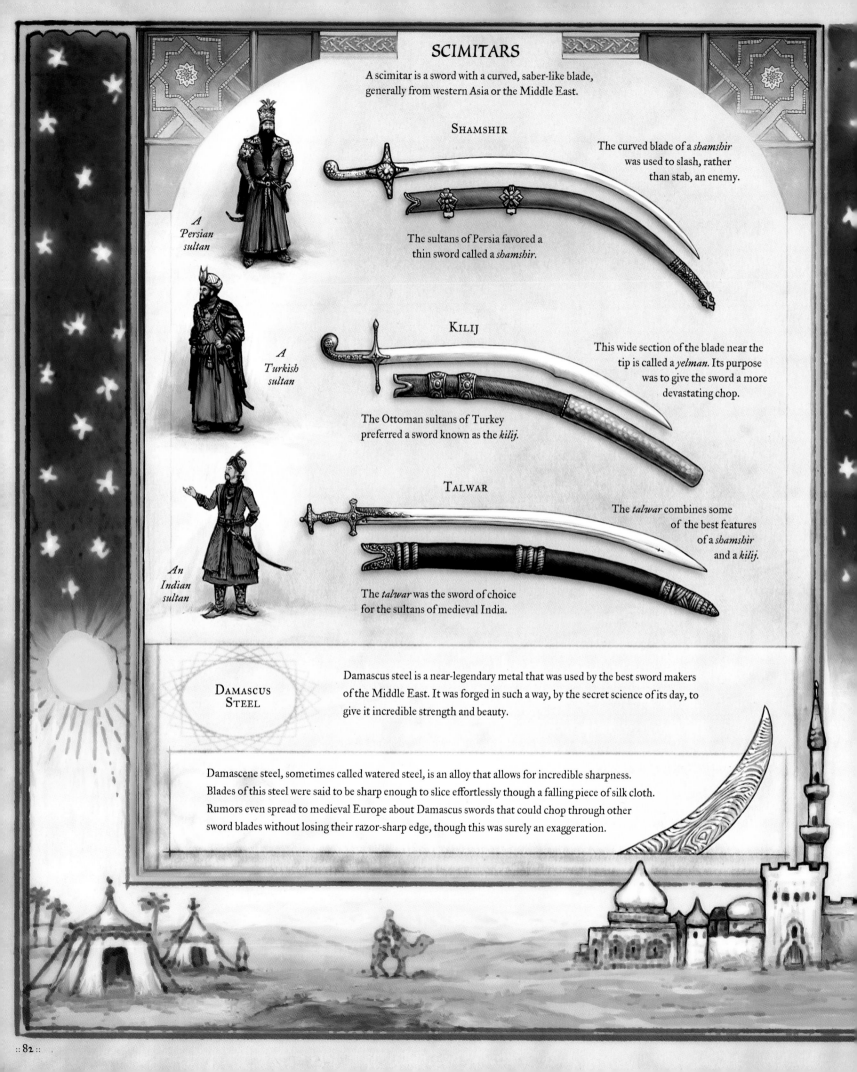

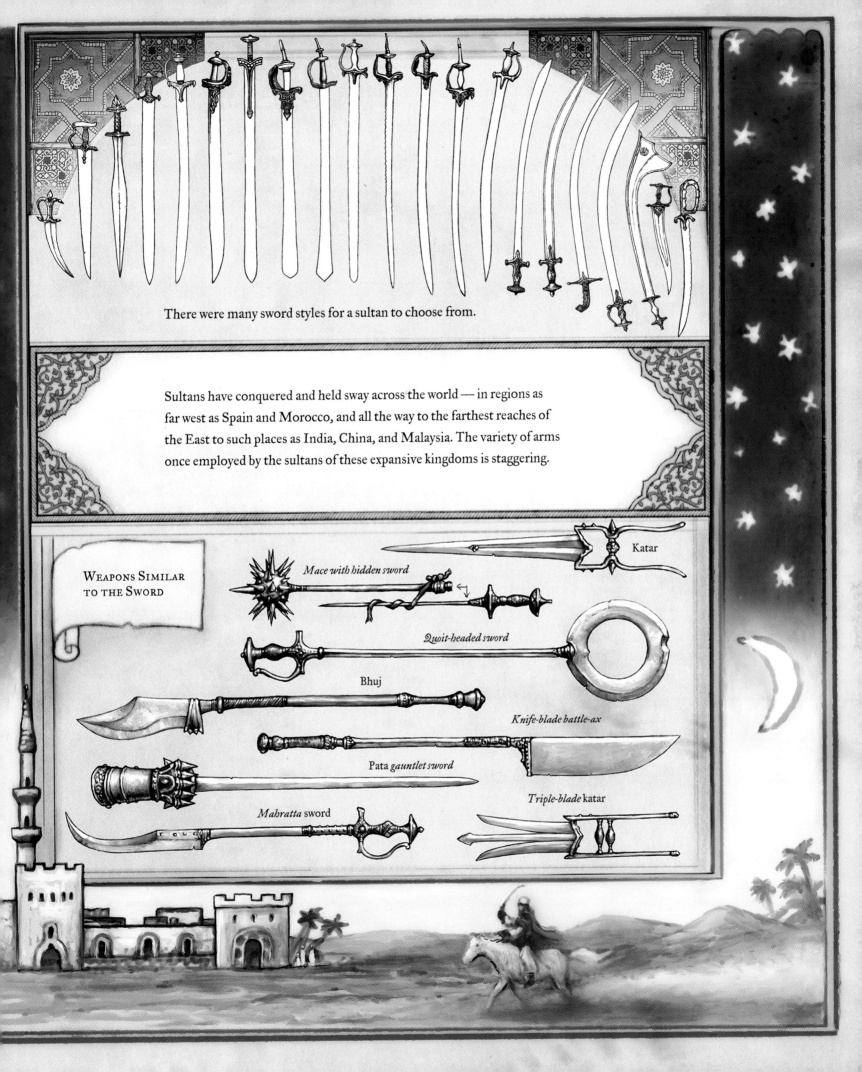

There were many sword styles for a sultan to choose from.

Sultans have conquered and held sway across the world — in regions as far west as Spain and Morocco, and all the way to the farthest reaches of the East to such places as India, China, and Malaysia. The variety of arms once employed by the sultans of these expansive kingdoms is staggering.

WEAPONS SIMILAR TO THE SWORD

Mace with hidden sword

Katar

Quoit-headed sword

Bhuj

Knife-blade battle-ax

Pata *gauntlet sword*

Triple-blade katar

Mahratta sword

Sources and Inspirations

This book was inspired by the work of countless swordsmiths, artisans, and craftsmen, ancient and modern, whose painstaking labors have created works of enduring beauty. I am also indebted to those scholars who have brought to light the achievements of days long past. In my efforts to explore the history of the sword, I tried to hew to historical accuracy — but in any artistic endeavor, personal interpretations are inevitable. Thus, I wish to make clear that any errors are my own and not those of my sources.

Select Bibliography

Burton, Richard F. *The Book of the Sword.* Dover Publications, 1987.

Clements, John. *Medieval Swordsmanship: Illustrated Methods and Techniques.* Paladin Press, 1998.

Duk-Moo, Yi, and Park Je-Ga. *Muye Dobo Tongji: The Comprehensive Illustrated Manual of Martial Arts of Ancient Korea.* Translated by Sang H. Kim. Turtle Press, 2000.

Earle, Joe. *Lethal Elegance: The Art of Samurai Sword Fittings.* MFA Publications, 2004.

Egerton, Lord of Tatton. *Indian and Oriental Arms and Armour.* Dover Publications, 2002.

Grafton, Carol Belanger. *Arms & Armor: A Pictorial Archive from Nineteenth-Century Sources.* Dover Publications, 1995.

Harris, Victor. *Cutting Edge: Japanese Swords in the British Museum.* Tuttle Publishing, 2005.

Hart, Harold H. *Weapons and Armor: A Pictorial Archive of Woodcuts and Engravings.* Dover Publications, 1982.

Hefner-Alteneck, J. H. *Medieval Arms and Armor: A Pictorial Archive.* Dover Publications, 2004.

Jwing-Ming, Yang. *Ancient Chinese Weapons: A Martial Artist's Guide.* 2nd ed. YMAA Publication Center, 1999.

Kure, Mitsuo. *Samurai: An Illustrated History.* Tuttle Publishing, 2002.

Miller, Douglas. *The Landsknechts.* Men-at-Arms 58. Illustrated by Gerry Embleton.
Osprey Publishing, 1978.

Miller, Judith. *Tribal Art: The Essential World Guide.* Dorling Kindersley, 2006.

Oakeshott, R. Ewart. *The Archaeology of Weapons: Arms and Armour from Prehistory to the Age of Chivalry.*
Dover Publications, 1996.

Oakeshott, R. Ewart. *Records of the Medieval Sword.* Boydell Press, 1991.

Oda, Hirohisa. *Real Ninja.* Ninja Publishing, 2002.

Peers, C. J. *Ancient Chinese Armies, 1500–200 BC.* Men-at-Arms 218. Illustrated by Angus McBride.
Osprey Publishing, 1990.

Peirce, Ian. *Swords of the Viking Age.* Introduction by R. Ewart Oakeshott. Boydell Press, 2005.

Richards, John. *Landsknecht Soldier, 1486–1560.* Warrior 49. Illustrated by Gerry Embleton.
Osprey Publishing, 2002.

Sato, Kanzan. *The Japanese Sword: A Comprehensive Guide.* Translated by Joe Earle.
Kodansha International, 1983.

Stone, George Cameron. *A Glossary of the Construction, Decoration and Use of Arms and Armor
in All Countries and All Times.* Dover Publications, 1999.

Turnbull, Stephen. *Ninja, AD 1460–1650.* Warrior 64. Illustrated by Wayne Reynolds.
Osprey Publishing, 2003.

Turnbull, Stephen. *Samurai Commanders (1), 940–1576.* Elite 125. Illustrated by Richard Hook.
Osprey Publishing, 2005.

Wei-Ming, Chen. *Taiji Sword and Other Writings.* Translated by Barbara Davis.
North Atlantic Books, 2000.

Yun, Zhang. *The Art of Chinese Swordsmanship: A Manual of Taiji Jian.* Weatherhill, 1998.

Zabinski, Grzegorz, and Bartlomiej Walczak. *Codex Wallerstein: A Medieval Fighting Book from
the Fifteenth Century on the Longsword, Falchion, Dagger, and Wrestling.* Paladin Press, 2002.